The Teachings of Jonah

The Teachings of Jonah

✦

The Medium for Jonah is Hossca
Harrison

*Transcribed and Edited by Constance
Luciano*

iUniverse, Inc.
New York Lincoln Shanghai

The Teachings of Jonah
The Medium for Jonah is Hossca Harrison

iUniverse books may be ordered through booksellers or by contacting:

iUniverse
2021 Pine Lake Road, Suite 100
Lincoln, NE 68512
www.iuniverse.com
1-800-Authors (1-800-288-4677)

Because of the dynamic nature of the Internet, any Web addresses or links contained in this book may have changed since publication and may no longer be valid.

The views expressed in this work are solely those of the author and do not necessarily reflect the views of the publisher, and the publisher hereby disclaims any responsibility for them.

ISBN: 978-0-595-47415-8 (pbk)
ISBN: 978-0-595-71082-9 (cloth)
ISBN: 978-0-595-91693-1 (ebk)

Printed in the United States of America

Contents

Foreword
by
Hossca Harrison

In September of 1981, I was hiking through the jungles of Central America with my business partner, looking to buy a hard wood forest. I soon found myself becoming ill with something quite similar to malaria. By the time I reached my home in Olympia, Washington, I had become so ill I could not function as president of my company, which developed land and built apartment buildings.

During the next two months, my physical condition continued to deteriorate. My family doctor ran test after test, but could not find a definite cause. He figured I must have contracted this illness from insects in Central America.

One evening while I was resting, sitting in an upstairs room of my lakeside home, I looked up and saw three "people" standing there facing me. They were wearing brown hooded robes, yet they were faceless. As they lifted their arms toward me, I sat up and pushed my back into the chair, as if through the chair! Then they disappeared.

I went downstairs and nervously told my wife, what had just occurred. "You must have fallen asleep and had a dream," she said. Yet I knew I had not fallen asleep. I continued to ask myself why this had happened. I was not a religious or spiritual person. In fact, I considered myself an atheist.

As I was preparing for bed, I decided to go sit in my whirlpool off the bedroom, to try and relax. As I was sitting in the water with my eyes closed, I was hit with a ball of white light on my forehead. With this, I began to see a vision of another time and place which I had never remembered seeing before. About thirty minutes passed before the vision began to fade. Then, all I could think about was to go to bed.

The next day I shared this experience with my family doctor. His reply was to go on a vacation, get out of town, go lay on a beach somewhere, and just rest. That afternoon my brother called to say there was a special in the paper for a trip to Hawaii for seven days. He suggested that the four of us go, my brother and I and our wives. That was it. We would go to Hawaii and just rest. And when I returned I could get back to the business of building apartments.

On the day of our departure I awoke with a case of gout. Never having had this before, I thought it had something to do with my illness from Central America, or my weakened spine from an earlier surgery. But nothing was going to stop us, and off we went to Hawaii.

While in Hawaii, the gout continued to get worse, where at times I had to be in a wheelchair. "Some vacation!" I kept thinking to myself.

On our last day in Hawaii my brother talked me into going out to the lagoon. "You can snorkel and get the weight off your foot," he said. "It will be good for you. Let's go!"

Off I went hobbling on one foot down to the lagoon. My brother was right. My foot did feel better, just relaxing, floating on the water. Then, I began to feel myself being pulled out. I tried to swim back to the shore, but with my foot throbbing with pain, I was pulled out further and further. Finally, I was pulled under. I could feel myself breathing in water. Suddenly, I was pushed to the surface, yet I was still not able to get any air into my lungs. Then I was pulled under again. A second time I was pushed up, and this time I was able to scream, "Help! Help!"

There appeared a large Hawaiian man standing on the coral ridge overlooking the lagoon, looking at me. He took off his shoes, ran barefoot across the coral, jumped in the water, and pulled me to the shore. By this time, my wife and brother were there, waiting for the Hawaiian man to pull me in. As I continued to spew water, the Hawaiian man looked at my wife and stated, "He will be okay." He then quickly disappeared.

Later, when the police took the report, the resort complex said there was no such person in the area. Hawaiians are not allowed at that resort unless they are wearing uniforms.

I was helped up to my room in the hotel. As I sat on the side of the bed in my room, I fell over and stopped breathing. My brother, who was standing there and saw what had happened, immediately called the paramedics.

The next thing I remember, I was floating up by the ceiling looking down at my body in a hospital, watching them jolt me with electric shocks. I thought to myself, "That must hurt," yet I felt nothing, physically or emotionally.

With that thought, I was pulled backwards at a high rate of speed up a long tunnel filled with light. When I came to the end, I was standing there looking at a being dressed in a white robe. His hair was golden and braided in a circle on top of his head. His eyes were pulsating shades of blue. Behind him were a group of people dressed in what looked like regular street clothes, but they were too far away for me to make out who they were.

Knowing there was a group of people standing there, my curiosity got the best of me. I wanted to find out who these people were. I wasn't interested in who this being was with the golden hair. So, I kept trying to walk around this being to see who these people were, and he kept moving and blocking me. Finally, he put his hand on my shoulder and said, "Now the work shall begin. Ye must return now."

The next thing I knew, I was coming out of a coma, but I had total amnesia. I didn't remember who I was, my wife, children, where I lived, what type of work I did, nor where I was. They took me by ambulance from the small hospital, at the north shore, to Honolulu, where they kept me a few days under observation. Then they released me to the care of my family doctor back in Olympia.

After six weeks of trying different methods, including being hospitalized again in Olympia, and then being lost by the hospital staff (I had slipped into a coma again and was misplaced by the hospital attendants), my family doctor made arrangements for me to see a psychologist in Seattle who utilized hypnotherapy.

After a couple of sessions under hypnosis my memory began to come back, or at least I could more clearly remember what all my relatives had been telling me about my life. When I returned for another session, I shared with the psychologist my experience while I was in a coma. He asked if I wanted to explore this further, with his guidance. I decided I did because I could not get this experience out of my mind. I knew I needed to put it to rest, and perhaps this was a way.

The following week I went back again and he put me under hypnosis. This time, while I was under, an entity which the psychologist could see as a cloud, walked into his office, entered my body, and began talking to him about his patients, their childhood histories, what true psychology was, and how to work with schizophrenics and multiple personalities. When I came out from under the hypnosis, I did not remember what had occurred, but I saw a very bewildered and astonished stare on the psychologist's face.

As the psychologist explained to me what had occurred, I thought, "Who's crazy here?" Something like this was the furthest thing from my mind.

The psychologist then asked, "Would you like to continue exploring this? I think it is important. And I do not want to charge you for this, for we are both learning from this experience."

As the weeks passed, the psychologist brought in groups of psychiatrists, psychologists, hypnotherapists, and counselors to ask this entity questions about their own lives and the lives of their patients. After several weeks, the conclusion was that it was a power higher than myself, but they couldn't describe exactly what it was.

During one hypnotherapy session, the entity who called himself Kitesa, told the psychologist that there would be a healing demonstration in a short time. The short time came to be the next week when I received a call from the psychologist's office.

The psychologist said, "I want to ask Kitesa if who I am thinking about is the one for the healing demonstration." The psychologist had received a phone call from the parents of a fourteen-year-old boy who was in the intensive care ward at a Seattle hospital and was given two weeks to live. The boy had been a patient of the Seattle psychologist for a couple of years but had not seen him for a year or so.

About twenty minutes after I arrived at the psychologist office, Kitesa came through. He said, "Yes. Go now to the hospital and we will send energy through the vehicle (me) to assist in the healing."

As we were driving to the hospital, I held the thoughts more than once, "Let's just turn around. I want to go home. I have apartments to build. I have had my share of hospitals."

But we didn't turn around. We arrived at the hospital. With the boy's parents' permission for me to work on him, we walked into his private room. I saw multiple tubes coming out of his body. I was told he had a strange blood disease. His blood would collect into pockets and not fully circulate through his organs. His organs were dying. The boy had already had part of his intestines removed. He was scheduled for an emergency operation, and his blood pressure was soaring at 300 over 200.

I began to hear a high-pitched voice in my mind, telling me where to put my hands and how to work on this boy. As I placed my hands on his chest and stomach, I could feel intense heat coming out of my hands. The heat generated from my hands was so intense, it left marks on my hands and the boy's chest and stomach for days afterward. The operation was canceled, and after two more visits with this boy, he walked out of the hospital.

After the second visit with this boy, the doctor on the case came up to me and said, "Look, I do not know what you are doing in there, and I do not want to know what you are doing in there, but it is working. Keep doing it!"

With that statement, I then remembered the rest of a message I received, to found a center where teens can be assisted.

In 1986, my wife, Rebecca, and I founded the Universal Education Foundation, a non-profit educational foundation to explore the healing powers in all of us, but mostly to work with teens. Since then, we have worked with teens, many of whom have been addicted to and dealing drugs. We work at helping them understand that there are powers of healing rather than destruction, and that there is the power to create a life of joy rather than a life of pain.

Rebecca and I are guardians of the Universal Education Foundation. We choose not to receive a salary. Instead, we support ourselves through the work with Jonah.

At one time when Kitesa was speaking through me, he said, "There shall be three that will prepare you for the strong teacher, then this teacher shall remain with you until your days on Earth have ended." The three were Kitesa, Alakanata, and Alunastar. Jonah arrived in 1984. Since then, Jonah has been actively working with many groups of people around the world. Whether Jonah is working with people in the United States, Europe, Australia, Africa, or South America, the questions seem to be the same, "Why am I here?" and, "How am I to do what it is I am to do?"

It is my hope that the information contained in this book can be of assistance to you in your life, as it has assisted people around the world.

As I have learned, whatever you do, do it in the Light.

—Hossca Harrison

For more information about Hossca's life, readers can find his book *Tide of Change* available on the Jonah Life Institute website, *www. jonahlifeinstitute.com.*

Introduction
by
Constance Luciano

This book was a labor of love, primarily created from an early series of taped messages by Jonah, a spiritual being in the non-physical, whose medium is Hossca Harrison. Jonah's teachings are universal and are about freedom, taking total and complete responsibility for who and what we are, and unconditional loving. His manner is direct and speaks to the heart.

This book project began with a vision I had in 1989, of providing the core teachings of Jonah in written form, making these teachings easily accessible to the general public. It is the first of what I originally intended to be a series of books stemming from Jonah's teachings. That vision still remains. It took extensive transcription and editing to develop the chapters for this book, which was first completed in 1991.

At Jonah's request this past year, I made additions to the original manuscript, enhancing the chapters with other messages from his continued tape and CD series to render the topics more complete. Although hearing Jonah speak is a wonderful experience, reading the material can provide a very effective means to assimilate and digest the information. In addition, much of the early information used in this book is no longer in circulation, not having been reproduced in years, thus augmenting the need to make this available now in written form.

I am honored to have compiled this work, editing it into the chapters for this book, and to have facilitated the accessibility of Jonah's message.

xvi   The Teachings of Jonah

Every effort was made to keep Jonah's words and the intent of his messages intact and as clear as possible.

Throughout this book, Jonah reveals who he is and why he has come to bring us his message. The following chapters were developed to provide a basic foundation of his teachings, with the last one leaving us with a beautiful vision of the Earth after the coming Earth changes. Here is a brief overview of what you will find discussed in the upcoming pages:

- Spirituality—how people place spirituality outside of themselves, what we need to recognize, and how to get in touch with our own spirituality.

- The prevalence of the fear-aspect of world consciousness, and how fear stems from the illusion of separation, plus tools to assist in releasing these fears.

- How the death experience is actually a birth into another reality, and how our thoughts and understandings in this physical life determine what type of reality we will be born into when we die.

- Healing—how disease is created and what the relationship is between the mind, the emotions, and the body.

- The meaning of the concept "Christed-consciousness."

- Insights into the power and abilities of the mind, and how the mind as a transmitter and receiver of thought forms is different from the brain.

- How meditation is a both a tool and a technique to assist us in reaching the core of the inner realm in which our chosen destiny lies.

- Sexuality in regards to the subconscious mind, and how, as an activity, sex is an exchange of energy which can bring an intensity of joy and union when understood.

- Human relationships—how to enhance the true bonding which we yearn for within ourselves, with our families, and with our loved ones.

- A.I.D.S—the correlation between the attitudes in the mass consciousness and the physical disease.

- How prophesies and predictions are made, and what they are.

- Future Earth changes and a beautiful vision of what these changes will eventually create.

I am delighted for all who have been drawn to read this book. May you be inspired and enriched by its powerful wisdom and may it be a phenomenal journey.

—Constance Luciano

1

Spirituality

Good day. Many identify us with the label "Jonah." We come from a dimension beyond your universe that is not physical, nor is it comprehensible to the human consciousness. It is a dimension of light, color and sound. We utilize the word "we" because we are not separated from all that is. We have come forth to your Earth to teach because we have been called. We have come forth to assist in the opening of the heart, to bring a message of freedom, of that which one is in truth, and of the freedom to come into expression of one's own power, one's own knowingness. We use the word "heart" as simply a symbol for the inner spirit, the inner soul, the part of you that connects you to the Universe. And the "Universe" is a symbolic word for all that is.

It is not our purpose to establish further belief systems, but rather to assist in releasing belief systems. For, in that release is when one's knowingness comes forth. When the knowingness comes forth, the freedom comes forth, freedom from fear, freedom from pain, and freedom from the illusion of separation. It is our purpose to bring an understanding of universal principles that bring joy, happiness, and peace within the individual to then be shared with brother/sister souls.

There is coming a time of change, the time of recognition that each individual, who is part of the whole, has the power to create change. And whatever that change is, however small that change is, however expansive that change is, it does affect the whole. You are not separate from the whole.

1

We have come to teach the human consciousness how to live, how to laugh, how to play, without living in the great serious mind of the adults of your world. So many in the human consciousness perceive spirituality as the great seriousness that discourages laughter, playing, and living. Many are so entrapped within this limited concept of spirituality and the terms of human development established by religions on your Earth that they live in fear, fear of a man-made god, fear of man-made rules and regulations that inhibit growth and the spontaneity of laughing.

What is spirituality? Many in your world proclaim that they know what spirituality is and how to achieve it. But we find many who are constantly placing spirituality outside of themselves, whether in man-made religions, such as Christianity, or in the great light centers that were established in Atlantean times to worship crystals. Many place spirituality outside of themselves without recognizing that total spirituality is the acceptance, the acknowledgment, and the belief in what is within one's own being, what is often called the heart. Total spirituality is the recognition that the heart, the soul essence, is an aspect of God and is not separate from God.

And the word "God" is an ancient word that truly has not been understood in the translation of your languages, particularly in your English language that loses so many meanings of the original words. The word "God" simply means creative force and/or creative source. What is there that does not create? Even an ant creates, a seed or flower creates, water, air and oxygen create, atoms and molecules create. All that is called God. God is not a singular being. It has been through the misconceptions of religion that has placed God as a singular entity outside of oneself, that would punish you if you do wrong or give you wings if you are obedient, for goodness sakes. The only punishment that exists is your own self-punishment.

Many have been taught self-judgment and condemnation, what is right and wrong, good and evil. Many have been taught to place labels on all that exists, and then to judge the labels. In truth, spirituality is learning how to laugh on the inside and how to play without fear of what the small minds of others would judge.

Souls who have chosen to physically incarnate on the Earth are choosing to create and to learn from their creations. The human mind is simply a tool. It is a tool used to create in the physical, a tool used to manifest and to experience one's own creations, whether they be positive or negative. When the mind is attuned to the world consciousness, it creates a negative environment. When your mind gives greater power and credit to the small minds of others that dictate how to live, when to live, and where to live, your mind is placing your own power outside of yourself. When you must run to this organization or that organization to find truth, or to find awareness, you are placing power outside of yourself. You become programmed to this state of consciousness which creates negativity. Your physical form then experiences negativity within this illusion.

But when your mind stops giving credit to the small minds of others, when your mind is attuned to the heart and soul, and follows the energy and direction of the soul, then you will experience living within a positive realm. You will be creating a positive environment. You will find true joy, and live and experience true joy.

Truth is simplistic. But many minds seek to complicate truth, to make truth incomprehensible to the masses. When people perceive they have all the answers, or have all the truth, or when they insist that you come and join their church, their religion, their light center, they are simply exercising a form of control and manipulation. In truth, a light center is just a drawing of souls of like mind, of like heart, who seek to live in the Light, and to live in the positive. Within a true light center there is no manipulation or control. There is no ego. When people seek to create an organization and place a label on it to justify their own ego and their own control and manipulation, be assured it is not a light center. When you look at many existing churches that proclaim you must belong to their particular organization and follow their doctrines to find truth, be assured that the church is not of truth.

Mankind has accepted the belief of limitation. In accepting this belief of limitation, the mind and the creativity of the heart is thus limited.

As the conscious mind looks at this illusion called Earth through the energy of limitation, it perceives this Earth as one reality. In truth, many realities and dimensions exist within the same space. But because the mind has accepted limitation, vision, knowing, and comprehension are limited.

What the mind believes, the body becomes. Often the mind will lie. The body does not. The body is a manifestation of the mind and mental processes. When the mind is in harmony with the heart, there is no disease, and the body does not live in trauma. When the mind lives in truth, the body will live in truth. The physical form will be in harmony.

Many on your Earth proclaim to be teachers. But a true teacher is one who lives one's own teaching. Those who call themselves teachers, who do not live their own teaching, are hypocrites seeking ego aggrandizement to create a fulfillment within the power structure of their own mind.

Many constantly ask, "Where can I find a teacher? What organization can I join? What religion can I belong to?"

You may as well ask, "How may I place spirituality outside of myself so I do not have to take personal responsibility for what I create?" Some would rather give responsibility to an organization or a hypocritical teacher than take personal responsibility for what they have created.

Within your culture of Christianity one came forth who was known as an avatar, a man named Jesus. Many recognize the label this one chose. But many within their limited state of consciousness take this master's teachings and manipulate them to place fear and control over others' minds to achieve desired results and to gain power over others. This one, called the master teacher Jesus, came to Earth with a teaching, a message. The message was one of total unconditional loving. Jesus did not say to judge one another. He did not say that one religion is better than another.

He did say that the religions which were in power at that time were teaching control and manipulation and hiding truth from the masses.

Jesus taught not to bow to the great laws that restrict and limit. Instead, he taught to recognize your own potential, to recognize your own loving, and to love others without judgment. He came to teach freedom to the human race. The human race did not listen. And they are still held in bondage, a bondage of limitation of their own minds and their own self-expressions.

Jesus came to teach how to live, how to laugh, and how to love without bowing to others. He taught that all that you see him do, you also can do. But you cannot do it by living and accepting the reality of limitation.

Jesus knew the many realities that exist on this Earth. He knew that this Earth is simply an illusion. If you hold the mind in limitation, you will not see beyond the illusion. You will become entrapped within the illusion.

Do you want to allow the illusion to control your mind? This is no different than if an artist painted a portrait and the portrait began speaking. Then, the artist began accepting orders from the portrait. The artist began bowing down and worshipping the portrait. Then, the artist allowed the portrait to control and manipulate, to indoctrinate the artist's mind. This is the same thing mankind does. Mankind looks into this illusion that itself has created, then it allows the illusion to control and manipulate through fear.

When you find someone who teaches fear, who places fear in the mind, you have found a person who teaches negativity, because fear is negativity. True spirituality, in simple terms, is learning to accept, to follow, and to love unconditionally one's inner knowing, inner being, and inner expression. Yet as many people so often place spirituality outside of themselves, they continue to live in trauma, sorrow, and pain. They continue having suicidal thoughts in the mind. They continue fearing others. They continue negating the inner self. This is total negation of the teaching of truth.

Truth, as we stated earlier, and we will state it many times, is simplistic. Yet the belief system commonly held is that truth is greatly complicated, that understanding spirituality is complicated, and that understanding the Light is complicated. Many teach that you must live in a specific location to be able to achieve spirituality, that you must live in this light center or that light center to find spirituality, that you must wear crystals, that you must wear crosses to find spirituality. Such negation of the heart! Search the minds that believe in this, that are constantly placing true spirituality and the awareness of the higher state of consciousness outside of themselves. These people believe in a very limited form. You do not need to do this. You do not need objects. You do not need geographical locations to find spirituality.

What is needed is total unconditional loving of one's own self, without judging in accordance to the rules and regulations that have been programmed into the mind since childhood, of right and wrong, of good and evil. Simply stated, it is a matter of accepting positive energy or negative energy. Within the heart lies all the ability to find spirituality. You will recognize this fact as you learn to begin quieting the mind from the great mental rhetoric that constantly runs in small circles, as you listen and have faith within yourself that you can do this.

What the mind believes, the body and mind become. Hold the concept in your mind that it will be very difficult to quiet the mind and listen to the heart, and you will have already created the difficulty in doing this. You will have held on to the belief structure, the energy, to do this and to block this. If you hold the concept in your mind that it is just as easy to quiet the mind and listen to the heart, you will program the mind with positive energy. Yet so often, mankind accepts negativity. People believe they cannot do this, they cannot do that. They limit their own ability and their own growth.

As many people hold on to the belief structure of karma, they lock themselves into the karmic wheel. Karma and negativity only exist when unconditional loving does not. But so many believe they must repay karma. This is a belief in self-punishment. And that will occur! Karma exists when unconditional loving does not. When you have accepted the responsibility of loving yourself unconditionally, karma does not exist. The master teacher Jesus also spoke of this, but much of it has been deleted by the many religious teachers of your world, the teachers of the world consciousness. Jesus taught that in total unconditional loving is the law of grace. He taught that living in a state of unconditional loving, which includes loving your own self, is living under the law of grace, and is releasing all karma, releasing all aspects of the negative consciousness. He who believes in karma experiences negativity.

It is important for the human consciousness to recognize that there is no true separation between what is physical and what is spiritual. The limited mind has believed in such a separation. Many continue to live in separation, restriction, and denial. And they wonder why there is pain in the heart. They wonder why there is depression, sadness, sudden shifts in personality, trauma constantly in the mind, constant crying, and constant sorrow. Yet they hold so tightly on to their beliefs. They find it hard to accept that achieving true joy is simple. All that is needed is self-loving and the releasing of judgment. Yet many respond, "This is so difficult. I can't do this. I've been judging all my life. How can I stop judging?"

Because they hold on to these cultural beliefs, they make it difficult to understand, to believe, to laugh, to live, and to enjoy the physical. The physical was not meant to be lived in suffering and denial. This has all been created by the teachings of small minds.

It is important to recognize what the human consciousness is. Think of the mind as a radio receiver and transmitter. The mind often dwells in negativity because the majority of thought waves that exist in your world are negative. When the mind accepts negativity as a reality, it absorbs these negative thought waves, much like your radio receives radio waves. The mind then transmits this energy through the human consciousness. It projects this energy of negativity, of constantly judging and condemning, denying loving, denying living and denying laughter. But when the mind dwells within a positive realm without judgment, without condemnation, it projects positive energy.

All thought is energy. All thought energy eventually manifests into physical matter. What the mind thinks, it becomes. What the mind gives power to, will rule the mind. It is a process of recognizing what is programmed into the mind, not just in the present, but throughout this lifetime.

Through a simple process, one can deprogram the negative energy in the mind. As negative thoughts enter your mind, all you need to do is make the statement in your mind that you do not desire the negative thoughts. Return to your Source. Constantly programming the mind to reject negative thoughts is the first step in reprogramming the mind to accept love, to accept yourself, and to accept the physical form into which you have chosen to incarnate.

Recognize that your soul is not separate from the Source, in truth. It is only the mind that has created interference. Coming into harmony with the Source is coming into harmony with yourself. Do this by restructuring the programming in your mind, between the attitudes of right and wrong, of good and evil, constantly holding the concept that you are a spiritual being on a pathway towards the Light and that there is not a power in all the Universe that can delay or stop this except your own mind. Recognize that there is nothing in all existence that has power over you unless you give it the power to control and manipulate your mind to hide from the heart.

Learn to love and to be loved. Learn to allow others to love you. Learn to stand up for what loving is, and to stop letting the dark minds of your world walk all over you, to manipulate and control you only to please their own egos. Such are the minds in your world that have been programmed as to what to accept and what not to accept, what is good and what is evil, what is right and what is wrong, simply to establish a level of judgment!

Come into harmony with the Source. Come into harmony with nature. Spend time walking in nature. Do not hold the concept in your mind that you do not have time for this. You do have time for this. Nature offers a healing energy to heal the pain and sorrow that so many in your world live in. Learn to please and to love yourself. Become at one with yourself. We have said this many times. And we will continue to say this throughout eternity because it is a truth that must be understood and lived. Loving yourself, accepting yourself, and recognizing the Source, are not things outside of yourself. All of this is within yourself. Do not place spiritual teachings outside of yourself, but within yourself.

We will not take responsibility for your creation but we will teach you as a soul, as a physical being, to take responsibility for your own creation. We will teach you how to create with love and positive energy, how to laugh, how to play, and how to become at one with the Source.

We do not desire a following, nor will we allow a following. It is not our purpose. Many people want this to flatter their ego. This is not our purpose. We are here to teach the mind and the heart. And we will never come forth to please the ego of the human consciousness.

For your own self, learn acceptance, learn loving, and accept the fact you can learn it. You can achieve it.

Constantly repeat to yourself in your mind, "It is easy to love, it is easy to laugh, and it is easy to play." Say these three statements in your mind each evening as you enter into the sleep state and you will find your environment changing. You will find your creation of negativity changing to a creation of light, beauty, and total unconditional loving. If it could not be achieved, we would not suggest it. It can be achieved. Know this. Accept this. Know yourself and accept yourself, because being a soul of the Light is being in harmony with the Source.

2

The Fear-Aspect of World Consciousness

A subject which greatly troubles this world is fear. The fear-aspect of the world consciousness cries of separation, denial, and limitation. It is important to recognize that the human consciousness is programmed from childhood with many limitations as well as programmed with many limitations from prior lifetimes that have been brought forth into this existence, this reality.

For a moment, stop and ask yourself why you carry fear. Why do you give the energy of fear such credit and such power over yourself? The first step in understanding and releasing fear is recognizing what you fear. And to come into recognition of this, is to come into an understanding that all thoughts held in the mind are energy. Thoughts create, and they create within this illusion. As you hold thoughts in the mind of a certain fear, either of the future, the past, or of others in the physical form, these thoughts are projected into the illusion, into the environment. The environment subsequently reflects back to you. It demonstrates fear to you. The illusion, the environment, is a direct manifestation and reflection of your own thoughts.

There is no such thing as a victim, a victim of fear, a victim of the environment, a victim of the illusion, or a victim of another person. But through holding and believing in the concept of fear, which is a negative energy, you will then bring this about within your own personal reality to experience, to live, and to recognize. What needs to be recognized in truth is that it is not meant for mankind to live in fear. It is not meant for this world to exist within the energy of fear, of limitation and denial. What also needs to be recognized is that many persons holding a great deal of negativity use fear as a tool. They use fear as a tool to gain control, to manipulate, and to separate. They use fear to divide the soul essence from the Source, the God-source, the God-within.

Recognize the many religions of your world that so greatly hold on to the doctrines of fear. They preach fear. They teach the fear that if you do not obey certain commandments of the priests, of the ministers, or of the rabbis, you would be condemned, the eternity of the soul would be in jeopardy. They teach this fear to keep many members within their congregations.

Do you realize that by living in fear you are creating circumstances, attitudes, environments, and events which will eventually totally destroy the physical body? The physical body functions closely with the mind. Each cell in the body is programmed by the mind, and when the mind is programmed by the world consciousness, the physical body will be a direct manifestation of world thought, of world attitudes.

As your medical professions seek to understand what creates cancer, running to and fro hunting for the many physical toxins, they hold on to a concept of the creation of disease which implies placing power outside of oneself. A disease is created by the mind. The mind creates the destruction of the physical body because of fear, because of denial, because of such restrictions in the mind. The mind creates disease by not allowing the true joy of the heart to be expressed, by not allowing yourself to play as a child. Disease is created by not allowing yourself to enjoy living and creating in the positive realm without carrying all the responsibilities of others. The responsibilities of others are not your responsibility.

Yes, my friends, take the time to begin searching in the mind for all the fears that you carry. Ask yourself what benefit it is to carry fear. Search for the passions that are created because of these fears. What joy is created?

What joy is recognized by carrying such fear in the programming of the mind?

And many will answer, "But I was taught fear as a child. Everybody has fear."

Because you believe everyone has fear, you have fear of having fear! Recognize that not only the conscious aspect of the mind, but the subconscious aspect of the mind is also being programmed to what is dictated by your societies, your governments, and your religions. The government is constantly preaching a fear that you may be attacked by another nation, that you would lose your freedom, that you would lose your identity. Do you have to acquire the greater weapons? The greater the manipulation, the greater control needed to honor the fear. The religions also utilize fear to place control over the mass mind. Some speak of heaven and hell. Some preach purgatory, the state in which there is not yet a decision of heaven or hell.

These fears must be released to allow universal tranquility, to allow the true joy of the heart to come into manifestation. Fear blocks the knowing of the heart. Fear blocks the knowing of that which is God. Fear can only exist when you negate the God-within, the child-within, the loving-within. Fear is but a sign that you are not following the inner self. You are not recognizing the inner self if you are giving the greater credit to what others think, what others do, what society dictates, and what the world dictates.

Is it not time to stop giving such credit to this world, to the world governments, and to the world religions? Is it not time to begin standing for justice, for the higher realms? Justice is taking total and complete responsibility for each thought you allow to enter into the mind, for each bit of programming you have accepted as a child, as an adolescent, as an adult.

We do not say that it is the parents' fault you were programmed, that it is the parents' fault that you carry fear, or that it is the parents' fault for this or that. Now is the time to recognize what the programming is. Now is the time to begin removing the old programming and old tapes of fear and limitation you have carried in the mind. So many on this Earth are crying in pain and misery because they choose not to take individual responsibility.

If you do not like your environment, the heartache, the pain, or the sorrow that constantly exists, then remove it. Be assured there is no one who will remove it for you. There is no one. This is an individual responsibility, an individual decision. And it must be a decision, not just a wish that it would go away. You worked at placing it in the mind. Now, work at replacing it. Replace it with positive energies, positive thoughts, and begin loving yourself.

There is such denial on this Earth. There is such denial of self-loving. Yet many state, "Yes, I love many people. I assist many." They would give their last dollar, their last peso, their last franc, or their last yen to someone. Yes, this is sharing with others, but it is not demonstrating that you love yourself. To love yourself is to give respect to yourself, to give respect to the God-within, to give respect to truth, and to respect that you do not need to live in negation or separation because of the energy of fear. You do not need to live in fear of what might happen to you, of what might happen in the future. The future is being created by the thoughts of the present. Continue your thoughts of the present and you will know what the future will be like.

There is an exercise you can do to assist in releasing the fears, limitations, and restrictions programmed into the subconscious mind when you were a child. To begin this process, recognize at which physical age you are presently. The exercise utilizes one week for each year of your age.

In the first week, meditate for a short period of time. To meditate, simply quiet the mind by either walking in nature, sitting alone in a room, or softly playing flute music (which would benefit some, not all). Totally relax the mind. And as you quiet the mind, as you close your eyes, mentally visualize your physical birth. Visualize in your mind the responses in your consciousness at the time of physical birth. Throughout this first week, journey from the physical birth to the first year of age.

Share with this child what in essence is your own subconscious. Share with this child that it need not fear anything in this lifetime. Share with this child that it is alright to love without limitation, and it is alright to be loved. Share with this child that limitation does not exist. Limitation is only a condition of your society and your world. Speak to this child. Tell this child it does not need to partake of the world consciousness, of the world manipulation and control. Speak to this child as you would a physical child. Love this child. And as you begin speaking and listening to the responses of this child, you will find certain limitations and automatic responses you have carried in relation to society, to individuals, to governments, and to religion, being released from the subconscious.

During the second week, visualize the child from the age of one to two. Recognize and ask this child what was programmed into the mind. What did the mind absorb and accept as gospel, as truth, as reality, that in fact was not? Listen to this child. Share your heart with this child.

During the third week, do the same for the third year of the child. For the fourth week, do the same for the fourth year, and continue this to the present age. And through each age, state to this child that you refuse to accept negativity. State that you refuse to accept pain, fear, negation, control and manipulation over the mind for the remainder of this lifetime. This would shift the tapes in the mind, the programming of the mind. This would begin the process of coming into harmony with the Source, with the God-within, and with universal tranquility. This would begin the process of allowing true joy and true harmony to exist.

Through living this example, you would assist others. And through others, others would be assisted. Dozens would be assisted. And then, hundreds would be assisted. Then, thousands and hundreds of thousands, and millions would be assisted. But before a shift of change can occur, it must begin in the individual. So many try to save the world without recognizing first they need to save themselves from their own world minds, not from the devils of the world, but from their own programming, and their own manipulation. To come into this understanding is the beginning of the understanding of truth.

It is important to begin recognizing what are the day-to-day activities in your life. Begin recognizing those with whom you speak, and those with whom you share. How many times when conversing with others do the conversations lead into fear, worry and frustration? Why do you not begin taking the initiative during these conversations to state to these individuals that by giving credit to worry, by giving credit to fear and the what-ifs, they are joining in a mass creation? When you agree with others about all the great worry and fear, then you have joined them in creating the fear. Together, you would both perceive the same reality and environment because you made a decision, a joint effort, to live in fear and to give your fear and frustration credit.

We say again to stand up and respect truth! Tell these individuals what they are creating with their own mind and their own thoughts. Teach what truth is. Also, recognize not to judge the individuals you are sharing this with. Do not hold the concept in the mind, "Well, they will not understand this." This is already establishing a preconceived judgment which then creates a blockage in the message. Also, do not judge their responses to your statements. It is your responsibility to state the message. It is not your responsibility whether they accept it or deny it.

And cease holding the fear, "If I speak this way, I will lose my friends." If you cannot share the heart, the feelings, and the knowledge, then they are not your friends. A friend of the heart will never depart. Always remember this.

Is it not time to stand up for truth? This society, this world, has existed in fear, negation, frustration, sorrow, pain and suffering to a point where the Earth is ready for a cleansing. You cannot teach or heal someone who does not desire to be taught or healed. Is it not time to recognize your own energy level, your own energy perceptions and to give credit to this and the greater loving, the greater acknowledgments?

Truth is loving. Through living this teaching you will attract friends of the heart who will not depart. You will attract ones who will love you as you love yourself. You will attract ones who will support you and whom you can support. Is it not time to take personal responsibility as a soul, as an aspect of God, and as an aspect of the Universe to begin assisting in the changes on this planet?

Do not misunderstand us. We are not stating for you to go out and save the world! You cannot do this because the world does not desire to be saved, particularly the world consciousness, world attitudes and world perceptions.

So many religions which teach fear speak of the return of the one called Jesus. They say he will take all of your problems, all of your burdens, and all of your fears. Have you ever stopped to consider that Jesus does not desire your fears? Nor does he desire your problems! But he does desire that you heed his teachings. When Jesus was in the physical, his teachings were not to follow fear, nor to be controlled and manipulated by religions and religious structures. He taught that you do not need to live in poverty. And he did not live in poverty, be assured! Jesus taught to release fear. He taught that there is only one commandment, and that is unconditional loving. Jesus taught acceptance of the Christ energy, which is unconditional loving, and which has no room for fear.

Do you seek to follow this one called Jesus? Then for goodness sakes, follow this one and not the world religions which control and manipulate through teaching the fear that you must remain as a member supporting their corporation!

To live truth is to speak truth. To speak truth is to live truth. Truth has many meanings on many different levels of consciousness. Each person carries his or her own individual truth. Each individual truth is the pathway a soul has chosen in accordance to the Source, to what is also called

God, or the Christ energy. This is the truth you need to follow. Recognize that not all souls have chosen the same pathway. There cannot be judgment because one soul chooses to learn one method and another soul chooses to learn another method. It is truth to each one, what each one is living, and the soul direction each one is following. You cannot make all the rules and regulations and say, "This is truth, and all on the Earth must follow this method to be in truth." This is a misconception based on the limitation of the human mind which exists in fear.

Many in your culture, civilization, and religions called fundamentalists teach such rules and regulations. They project and teach the fear that if you do not believe in the Lord Jesus, then you are condemned to hellfire, regardless of whether you live in jungles or tribes that do not have the media, for example. These are condemned to hellfire? Recognize that the teachings of fear that exist in your society are being taught to a greater degree to remain in control. Do not give these credit. They have no power over you unless you give them the power. We are not saying to judge those who are called fundamentalists. They are also loving. But be assured they will learn with much pain because they continue to live in separation. All religions, all governments that teach separation and denial will learn through pain. This is because pain only exists when you consciously choose not to follow the heart.

All of you have the ability to listen to the heart. Many of you state, "It is so hard to quiet the mind. It is so hard to meditate. How do I know when I am listening to the heart?" Because you hold the perception in the mind that it is difficult to do this, you have created the environment and the illusion that makes it difficult in order to prove your own mind correct. In the greater truth it is simple. All truths are simplistic. It is only the complicated controlling mind of man which places barriers, restrictions, and limitations, such as believing you need an interpreter for understanding truth. Search for interpreters and you discover you can buy an interpreter anywhere. But you cannot buy truth. You live truth.

We have come forth to your Earth plane through this physical body to teach freedom, freedom of expression, freedom of living, and freedom of loving. We have come to this Earth to teach what the Christ energy is. Many seek a label. What do we teach? How do we teach? We teach what some would call the teachings of Melchizedek. We have come to assist the mind of man to live in freedom, to release judgments, and to begin breaking apart the world consciousness so that true joy may finally be lived and recognized, that true loving may begin existing on this Earth. But because mankind has separated itself from the Source, from the Christ energy, from unconditional loving, it has lived in fear, it has had to run around trying to find its own savior, run around trying to find that which is not.

We have spoken on this Earth through many physical forms in many cultures, times, and dimensions to teach, although we have not taken a physical form through the birth process. We will continue teaching. We will continue speaking until mankind recognizes it can no longer live in separation and denial, until mankind recognizes it is an aspect of God regardless of what the world religions dictate, and until mankind recognizes that fear is the greatest blockage that exists in the human consciousness.

Fear is an establishment of being separated, of not having faith within your own self, within your own heart. Many preach and dictate they have faith in their religion, they have faith in their government. How many have faith in their own living, their own laughing, or their own beingness? How many have faith that they are of God? How many have faith that instantly you can come into recognition of the God-within, release fear, and reprogram the mind from negative to positive? How many have the faith that you can love yourself unconditionally regardless of how many times it was spoken to you as a child that you were not worthy of being loved, that you were a bad boy or a bad girl and you deserved to be punished, that you deserved to have pain? And you believed it! You believed it because your state of consciousness as a child consciously perceived you did not know any different. The soul did. But this is not an excuse for the present.

Those who have chosen to listen to this message take a responsibility. They take a responsibility for truth, of changing the programming in the mind, of changing and releasing the fear they have carried for so many years. The body does not need to exist in disease. Cancer does not need to exist. Heart disease does not need to exist. What you call breakdowns do not need to exist. What you call disabilities do not need to exist. But they do exist because you believe and give credit to their existence, and you fear them. For people who carry fear in the mind that they would develop cancer, be assured that if they continue living in this fear, they will physically develop cancer because they will be creating it with their mind. They create it with their thoughts.

Many of your doctors say that cancer runs in the family. Cancer does not run in the family. The state of consciousness runs in the family! As your relatives have lived in fear, they have taught you how to live in fear. Of course, you would carry the same disease. You carry the same consciousness.

Recognize that you have the ability and the knowledge to enter into freedom, freedom which creates true joy and true harmony. So many fear what is called physical death. But again, much of the teachings of the fear of physical death come from the religions of your world. What did you achieve? The gift of going to heaven? Or the judgment of going to hell? There is such a fear of physical death, of what would occur. Is the devil going to find you? Many do not recognize that within the world religions the devil has already found them! What is called the devil is simply negative thoughts. A satanic attitude is one of negative thoughts, of judgments, of fear, of negation, of separation, and of not following the pathway of one's soul. The devil you fear already has its grip on you when you live in separation.

When truly living the pathway of life, of truth, of the heart-way, and of unconditional loving, all fear dissipates. There is no room for fear when you live in truth. Physical death is no more than a physical birth. Upon physical death, you are simply born into another dimension of time, space, and reality. The soul never stops growing for all eternity. The soul never ceases learning. There is no such point where a soul will learn certain lessons, abilities, levels of consciousness in physical form, and then ascend into the Light and go on its retirement. Learning exists for eternity, in all dimensions, all realities, and all times.

In this time frame, your society is in great need of learning what fear is and is not, what limitation is and is not, what separation is and is not. Cease accepting the teaching of the psychiatrists, psychologists, and others of the world mind who dictate fear is normal to a certain degree. It is not normal. It is normal to live in true joy. It is normal to have fun living, to enjoy living. It is not normal to worry about tomorrow, yesterday, or today. Living in separation is not normal. But living in unity, at one with the Source, with the God-force, with the Christ energy, is normal.

When what is truly normal does not exist, much trauma is created. Cease believing in the concept that you need to be punished. Cease believing in the concept that you need to fulfill negative karma. Negative karma only exists when unconditional loving does not. Cease punishing yourselves. Cease all the great worry. And recognize that the Universe provides all that is needed when you follow the pathway of the soul. Stray from this and you will constantly battle. You will constantly need to fight because you will be living in separation, which is a negative energy. Separation is a hostile energy, a dark energy.

Fear has such a destructive nature. It creates separation from what one truly desires to create. Fear will lower the immune system and create disease. It creates pain, sadness, and depression. It inhibits growth. What you fear you draw unto yourself. When you learn to release fear, you can heal whatever difficulty you have mentally, emotionally, and physically. You can heal it.

Give credit to truth. Give credit to loving unconditionally. Do not sit in judgment of the religions, but recognize their teachings. Do not sit in judgment of the governments, but recognize their activities and that you do not need to be a part of them. Do not sit in judgment of your neighbor, but recognize what he or she is creating. Do not sit in judgment. It is a negative energy.

Judgment is a condition of the human mind. Judgment comes from a state of mind that seeks to control out of fear. If you judge, you empower the negative. Whatever that event is, whomever it is, if you are making a choice to judge it, and we use the word "judge" in terms of condemnation, if you condemn it, you empower it. Whatever you judge, you are giving power unto it and making it stronger. And when you empower it, you are disempowering the self. Then that event begins controlling your life.

Do not confuse the words "judgment" with "discernment." Discernment is of great importance. It is always your responsibility to discern what is appropriate for you in the moment, what will create the greatest loving and learning for you. It is always your responsibility to discern. When we use the word "judgment" we are using it in a totally different context. When we use the word "judgment" we are using it in terms of condemnation, of condemning.

Ones have a tendency to judge what they fear because on one level they know it reflects something in themselves they are not wanting to look at. When you are not wanting to look at something, fear is the result. When you are willing to look at that something, then there is no room for fear to come in. When you are willing to look at it, it pushes out the fear. The majority of your world is controlled by fear. Truly, every difficulty you carry in the mind was founded from fear. When you disempower yourself, you fill yourself with fear that only builds on top of more fear, and then more fear.

Recognize the free-will choice that exists. Recognize the free-will to choose pain or joy. It is your free-will choice. It is your decision. The decision will be made by no one other than you. While you cannot force anyone to change, you can teach and assist others to change. And remember, a teacher is not a teacher unless that teacher lives his or her own teaching.

Recognize that you live in the physical, you live on this Earth, and that this Earth is an illusion which reflects your own creation. You do not need to live in pain. You need not. And what is called the Christ energy, also called Melchizedek, and also called God, has no desire for you to live in pain and punishment. In truth there is no god who punishes or condemns, regardless of beliefs. There is not. The only god who sits in judgment and teaches and preaches fear and damnation is a creation of the mind of mankind. It is not a god of truth. Do you seek to worship a god? Then worship a god that loves unconditionally! But first, worship your inner self, the God-within. This is not ego. This is unconditional loving. This is recognition. This is sharing. This is coming into harmony.

Recognize the great absolutes of this world and the great absolutes of science that are often preached, whether it is how diseases are created or that fear is normal, for example. So many absolutes are preached by ones who think they know truth. In reality, what they think is only what they were taught by a limited mind. Recognize that there are no absolutes. For us to teach an absolute would mean there is no free-will choice. And there is always in existence your own conscious free-will choice, and you own soul essence free-will choice, although sometimes the two collide with each other. There are no absolutes in all there is.

3

Death—The Process of Life

The word "death" creates such fear, even for those who would perceive themselves as enlightened. Many people are confused and fearful about the departure from the physical. Understand that death is the same as birth. The death experience is a birth into another reality. We are choosing to speak on the subject of death to assist in understanding how in this physical life, this physical existence, and this physical form you call a body, you are choosing and determining what reality you will be born into when you die.

Many of the religions of your lands teach fear of death. Have you been good? Have you been bad? Will you go to heaven? Will you go to hell? Will you go to purgatory? Many religions teach a fear of judgment, fear of being condemned by God to a fiery hell where the devil exists and the demons exist.

We will also speak of those who have had near-death experiences, or what some would call a medical death, but yet the body lived again and certain memories were brought back. The majority of the memories were of ascending to a light, of an incredible peace, joy, and tranquility, and of meeting again ones they loved so dearly from the heart.

Others who have had this experience were terrified of the visions they saw. They perceived they were being chased by a devil. They perceived they were living in a hell, confirming their belief of a heaven and hell. They returned to ask great forgiveness from a god for their sins, so that when they do die they will not have to go to this place called hell. The majority reading this message do not believe in the concept of heaven and hell as a literal geographical location. But some do. Therefore, we will speak of both issues here.

Heaven and hell are simply states of consciousness, states of being. The difference between true joy and pain, disease, and depression is what is experienced in the physical plane. However, those states of consciousness do not solely exist in your physical plane. There are also states of consciousness called heaven and hell in the non-physical plane. Heaven would be described as experiencing a universal consciousness of freedom, tranquility, the exuberance of life, and the tranquility of laughter. Hell would be considered a state of being in which exist ghosts, or what certain religions call demons.

These so-called ghosts or demons are souls, entities, who do not carry a physical form, yet are entrapped in the Earth plane. They have not ascended to the Universal Light, to the Christed-consciousness. And we are not speaking of the word "Christ" in terms of the religions of mankind, which are invented by mankind. The word "Christ" represents a universal energy, which simply means unconditional loving, just as the words "Satan" and "devil" simply mean the denial of life, the denial of loving of oneself. The word "demon" simply means following a negative pathway, a negative attitude. "Heaven" means following the soul pathway of light, of truth, of the universal consciousness. They are all states of mind.

The mind exists beyond your physical existence. The mind is not the brain. The mind is an energy field which rests on top of the head. It is an electromagnetic energy field. The brain is a physical organ in the body structure which receives electrical impulses from the mind to control the body, to operate the body. Therefore, the mind is not physical substance. But the mind does work through the physical plane by directing energy wavelengths to create physical matter within your illusion.

Your mind creates your illusion. Your mind attracts to you what you have attracted to the mind. It is one and the same. There is no separation here.

What you call death is so greatly feared. The first aspect of the death process affects the physical body. But you need to understand that you have seven bodies. You have the physical body, the astral body, the mental body, and the emotional body, all four of which are attached to the Earth plane through the creative process of the illusion. You also have the etherical body, the Christ body, and the soul body, all three of which are connected to the Universe. When a blending of these seven bodies is in harmony with the physical mind, the mind which works in this physical plane, you have the ability to utilize and understand universal truths, universal concepts, and universal harmony. When these seven bodies are in alignment, disease does not occur. Depression of the mind does not occur. Pain does not occur.

Through the death process one will certainly dissolve one's physical body, but one's memories, emotions, and personality are not dissolved. The physical body is simply like clothing wrapped around the other bodies as a tool to manifest, to learn, and to teach in this physical plane of existence.

It is important to understand that there is no escape. Some of you who are reading this message may sometimes allow thoughts to run through the mind about committing suicide because you perceive the pain is so great. You perceive the loss you experience as a great loss. The depression is so great you cannot bear it anymore. You would desire to commit suicide.

Would you desire to kill the self? Surely, you have the free-will choice and the ability to do so. But first, you need to understand this truth: those of you who contemplate suicide, who have the ability and the power to dissolve the body, need to know that if you do this for the purpose of escapism, all of the pain you carry, the physical pain as well as the emotional and mental pain, will still be with you. Indeed, the physical body will be gone. It will dissolve back into the dust of the ground. But the pain which was carried in the physical body is still carried in the emotional body and in the mental body.

As we said earlier, you carry your memories with you. And the memory of that pain is still your reality. Understand that you are not a victim. The mental trauma and pain you are carrying, the physical pain you are carrying, you created. Understand that you are the one who must resolve it. No one can do it for you, regardless of whom you choose to follow. There is such a tradition in your land of searching for one to follow! Understand that no one will take your pain or your disease from you. Also understand that there are many who will assist you to any degree you request when you request from the heart to end the pain and the depression.

But you must be willing to receive the assistance. You must be willing to release the judgments. You must be willing to release the hatred you have carried about yourself. You must be willing to love yourself unconditionally. And to love yourself unconditionally is to accept your Christ body. The Christ body carries this ability. And when you make the statement that you cannot love yourself, that it is too difficult to love yourself, you are making a statement which is denying your own Christ-self. By denying your Christ-self, you are denying the assistance of the Universe, and you are accepting a reality of pain, of depression, and of separation. Separation of any one of these bodies will create disharmony in your illusion and your reality.

The soul body is an energy form that comes in many sizes. The size of the soul body expands and contracts according to your own vibratory level. The higher your vibratory level, the higher or larger the expression of this energy, or the larger the form you would perceive of the soul body. And this is true of all the bodies. Likewise, a body ridden with disease will often contract, will hold within, will lodge and lock within itself many toxins within the cellular structure of the physical body.

The lower the vibratory energy, the more contracted the energy is. The more contracted the energy is, the more you deny the assistance available to you. But understand that there is no one, physical or non-physical, who is not worthy of assistance from the God-force of the Universe, from the Christ-force of the Universe. Everyone has available to himself or herself all of the assistance of the Universe that is needed to create a healing in totality. It does not matter whether it is a disease of the body or the mind. Truly, there is no separation here. But you must be willing to ask for, and be willing to receive, the assistance available to you.

It is not difficult to receive this assistance. All one needs to do is ask and allow this energy of lovingness to be received. Many say they ask but they do not receive. Indeed, many do ask, but they are not willing to receive. Ask yourselves these questions: Are you willing to receive? How much are you willing to receive? How much negativity are you willing to release to allow room for the positive energy to be received, for the assistance to be received?

It is very important to understand that not one soul is ever lost. Indeed, it is important to allow yourself as a physical being to become enlightened to the universal truths, the universal joy, the universal tranquility, the universal peace, and the universal truth. The more enlightened you are when you choose to depart the physical plane, the higher the vibratory level you will be, and the more understanding you will have of the reality you have chosen to exist within as a being. As we have said before, you choose your reality that you are going to be born into, even before the physical death. The physical death is only the ending of one particular school. Indeed, no entity ever ceases in learning, ever ceases in growing, ever ceases in understanding unconditional loving.

Your words are greatly limited to describe the tremendous joy that exists in the Universe. But when people hold an attitude that they can kill their body to escape from the pain which they themselves created, and transcend to this great Light and universal joy, they are mistaken. There is no escape. By quitting school early you are not instantly in the higher level of learning. If you quit school, you return to school to learn what you chose not to learn. Those who do choose suicide indeed will return to the Earth plane.

The fears you carry in your consciousness when you commit this act of suicide, are the fears you will create as your reality in the non-physical state. This is very important to understand. What you fear, you will experience in totality in the non-physical state. What you fear you will also experience, whether you die of a disease or an accident, for example. The energy of fear is an energy of darkness. The energy of fear is an energy of separation and negativity. But remember, there is nothing to fear.

We understand well the human emotions that cry in trauma, sorrow, and loss, when a beloved one departs the physical. We understand the crying, the guilt, when you think you should have said what you never did say, the trauma based on your belief that you will never again see this beloved one, that you will never again hold the love of this one close to you. This is not true. Indeed, the physical form, the physical tissue of the body is gone, even though some try to preserve it. And why? To make an idol out of it? To place it within gold boxes, silver boxes, oak boxes, concrete boxes? To place it in the ground to fertilize the ground? Such is how the human mind is so attached to physical objects! And that is all a body is. A body is a physical object, a physical tool to utilize, to learn from, and to grow with. But understand that you will see your loved ones again. There is never a loss. It does not exist.

The loss of memory does not exist. The beloved mate who has departed, the beloved child who has departed, the beloved parent who has departed, you will indeed see this one again. True loving comes from the Christ body. The Christ body cannot be destroyed. It is an energy. It is memory. It is action. It is the creativity of love and of unconditional loving.

Love is never forgotten. Reuniting will always be. When you see the death of a beloved one, friend, family member, relative, understand that they have chosen to enter into another reality to allow their learning process to continue through eternity. Never is there a loss. A loss does not exist.

When one is truly enlightened to truth, to universal principles, the death process is a time of jubilant joy. It is a time of festivities. It is a time to truly hold a festival of joy, of laughter, of dancing. It is not a time for sorrow, to cry, or to weep. Allow tears of true joy to truly be. Understand there is never a loss. When you allow the energy of fear to be so ingrained, so imbedded in your consciousness, imbedded within the mental and the emotional body, then the mental and the emotional body do not ascend. Consequently, the mental and emotional body stay within the energy of the Earth plane creating a reality of that fear which is much more intense.

One who departs the physical in intense fear will experience that fear magnified in the non-physical state, but earthbound. That entity will not have ascended. But also understand that there are masters who utilize the Christed-consciousness of unconditional loving to assist such an entity in the non-physical state, to teach that fear does not need to be a part of one's creation, of one's experience, of one's reality. Thousands of earthbound entities daily ascend to the Light to raise their vibration, or re-enter the physical state to again learn the art of taking total and complete responsibility. As we have said many times before, never is there ever a soul lost.

We will now speak on the subject of physical children who depart the physical. We understand in totality your human emotions of the trauma, the fear, the loss of holding that physical form, the physical body you called your child. We also understand in totality those of you who hold fear and guilt over the death, the physical departure of a physical child. Understand there is not one singular answer for all incidences where a physical child has left through physical death. There is, indeed, an explanation for each. It is not our purpose to provide all of the explanations. It is our purpose to describe the most common, as you would perceive it.

One of the most common explanations is when a child will choose to leave the physical for a purpose of teaching. It is not to punish. It is to teach. It is to allow the raising of questions in the consciousness such as: What is life? What is death? What is loving? Thus many people are set on a pathway to begin truly searching the meaning of life, to allow their own growth to develop, and to excel beyond the limitations which they have previously accepted. Understand that whether you are in the physical or the non-physical, you will again see that child, be with that child, and communicate with that child.

And we are using the word "child" because it is a concept you hold in the mind in accordance with the physical form. Simply because the physical body is in the form of a child does not mean the soul essence is a child. The soul essence could have been a master or a teacher who came to teach a specific lesson. Each soul chooses a length of time in which to remain in the physical. But this length of time is not an absolute. It can be shortened or lengthened by decisions made in the physical and non-physical.

To understand the death of children and the teaching, allow yourself to absorb the teaching, to absorb the understanding of what is eternal life. Your English word "eternal" is so greatly limited. There is no ending because life never ends. It simply changes form. Always remember this.

From time to time, certain entities choose to incarnate in the form of children, as infants, where prior to the physical existence of this incarnation there existed degrees of fear of becoming lost in the physical state and the physical illusion. In these cases, souls sometimes make a decision, after a brief incarnation, to depart the physical because they perceive they are not yet ready. There is no judgment on this; right, wrong, good, or bad. There is no judgment. Your medical sciences often refer to this as "sudden infant death syndrome." When this occurs, do not perceive there is something wrong with you.

In every individual case called death there is a teaching, when your attitude allows yourself to be taught it. We are not speaking of just an intellectual understanding that life is eternal, but a true inner understanding. Life does not end. It simply changes reality. And often when a physical child departs the Earth through a physical death, and the lessons needed to be learned by the parents are learned, that same soul will again reincarnate as a child to these parents to continue the process of learning, of teaching, and growth here. What is always involved here is free-will choice, particularly the free-will choice of the parents to release the fear of loss and to understand and allow the growth that can be truly present through this.

Whatever organ is affected by a disease of those who are perceived as terminally ill, those who carry a disease called cancer, a disease of the heart, or a disease of the brain, simply indicates what attitude created the disease. Every organ of the body represents a particular attitude. We will speak further of diseases and attitudes, and the correlation between the two, in a different chapter.

Your scientists and spokesmen of your medical professions try to preserve a physical body at all costs. There are many physical bodies attached to your machines where the blood is flowing, the heart is pumping, and no soul exists in that body. You are simply maintaining the clothing because of the great attachment to the clothing. It is not beneficial to seek to prolong what you would call a terminal illness. We are not saying one should decide for another. We are stating it is not the decision of others. It is a decision of the consciousness. And for those whose consciousness is not present, let it be known they have made their decision. They are not seeking to return.

Even through death by disease, growth has been created. But if you perceive you can escape the disease by death, you cannot. There is no escape. There is only resolution.

Indeed, the biological chemistry of the disease has perished through death. The attitude that created it must also be healed because that attitude does not die with the body. The diseased, the living organism of disease is gone, but the attitude is not. And if that attitude is not released, and you as an entity choose to reincarnate in another form, the disease will surface again, often in your own childhood.

Many ask why innocent children carry diseases. Why do innocent children carry cancer and brain tumors? Why are infants born with deformed hearts, deformed brains, deformed limbs? This occurs because often the attitude in a prior existence was not healed. They left the body to escape from the disease. They did not allow the attitude, which is a level of consciousness that carries a level of energy, to be healed. They reincarnated before healing this. And again, the same energy manifested in physical form. Your level of consciousness will be represented in the physical form you carry whether it takes you one lifetime to resolve it or ten thousand lifetimes. There will come the opportunity and the time to finally resolve it. The opportunity is given each and every time. It is not always chosen.

However, this is not an absolute. We are not stating here that every infant and every child who carries a disease does so because they did not resolve their own issues in a prior existence. The majority of the time this is correct. But also understand that certain entities or teachers will incarnate and choose what you, in your language, would call a deformed body to create a teaching, to create an awakening of your own consciousness to learn to love unconditionally.

The majority, not all, but the majority of persons with Down syndrome, which science understands have a problem with the chromosomes, are here to teach unconditional loving. Those of you who turn away from individuals with Down syndrome out of fear, out of disgust, out of anger, do so because of your inability to love. When you see an individual with Down syndrome, embrace him or her. Embrace the individual with a hug. Speak of loving and watch yourself grow! Watch yourself come to an understanding of the immense love you are capable of achieving through the utilization of your Christ body.

By allowing this, you are healing yourselves of all negativity. The Universe does not judge. Judgment is a condition of the human mind. The Universe does not preach fear because the Universe does not preach. The Universe simply assists, guides, and directs.

There are many events to come to your world, and many will begin creating a desire of suicide. That is why we have spent time speaking of this. Suicide will not give you the escape you desire. Many events which will occur in the third dimension are events we prophesied two thousand years ago, events we prophesied over thirty-seven thousand years ago, of your time of existence.

What was called Lemuria is coming to be. The Christed-consciousness is returning unto awareness. There is coming a graduation, a movement of energy, and there is greatly needed the rapid movement of bringing your technology and spirituality into balance. If spirituality does not move rapidly enough to become equal with technology, technology will reverse to become equal with spirituality. Now is the time of resolution, of healing.

We have chosen again to return to this plane of existence to assist in enlightenment, to assist you to become your own master of your own reality. Be assured we have not come to create a following. By creating a following, one is not creating freedom, but oppression. We have come to teach freedom. We have come to teach you to take responsibility. And we have come to show you a way in which you do not need to experience the cataclysms coming to your world. We are offering you a pathway of freedom. Not one of you reading this message needs to experience the cataclysms to come. But for those of you who are choosing to experience it, so be it. You will grow. You will learn.

Truly, there are two methods of learning in your reality: one of pain, and one of joy. You have the power and free-will choice to choose. Those who make the decision to learn through true joy we will assist to the minuteness of the details of assistance so that you may grow to learn you are God. Truly, there is not a great difference between what is called the I, the Jonah, the I-am-that-which-I-am, and you. We know who we are. You are seeking to find who you are. Therefore, we have chosen to assist you to find who you are so that you too can be an I-am-that-which-I-am and know it, and not guess.

The process of death is a natural process. Yet there are those in your world who are teaching you to learn to take the body with you. For what purpose is this? Is it because people are so attached to the physical, and to the physical body, that they must learn how to preserve it? Are not the great morticians of your society already preserving the bodies? We well understand the difference in the philosophy here. One is seeking to create monies to preserve a body. Another is preserving the body out of fear of releasing a body. So be it. Understand that a physical body is like clothing wrapped around the soul.

The seven bodies we spoke of previously are all growing in this reality, not just the physical. Each body carries different attitudes in different vibrations of development. For all bodies to come into harmony, the low-est vibration must match the highest vibration. Then, the physical body has the ability to be, live, and exist as a soul. Those that speak of out-of-body experiences have the ability to travel without the denseness of a phys-ical form. But understand that you always travel without a physical form. You do not always remember it, but you always do it. The remembrance gradually comes and filters through the subconscious to the conscious mind when you are ready for that teaching. Seek to force it and you will block the teaching. Allow it and all the wisdom of the Universe is yours.

Learn to sing and dance and play. Indeed, this is the time of joy for life. For death is life. Death is the process of life. Without death, there is no growth.

4

Healing

Coming to understand the word "healing" is coming to understand the totality of your own beingness. You need to understand not from the intellect, but from the heart, the spiritual essence within you. You need to understand there is no separation in all that exists. When the mind begins separating and dividing, it creates confusion about what the heart is, the inner spirit, and the universal God essence of all universes. And when one creates such an energy of confusion, one begins entering into a state called disease.

Your English word "disease" means that one is not at-ease with oneself. There are blockages, and there is a separation existing in the mental body or the emotional body which begins manifesting sooner or later in the physical body. When one creates a disease in the physical body, that is the last stage of manifestation. This means that the difficulty which brought on the disease has been there for some time creating pain in the mind, pain in the emotions, and then the pain in the body.

There are those of you who truly desire to be healed. And there are some who do not want to be healed. There are some whose minds delight in their own affliction. But also understand, those who want to hold on to the disease are not always aware consciously they are wanting to hold on to the disease. To create a healing, one needs to come to an understanding of all parts of oneself. Where did the energy, the separation, begin occurring? Where did the blockage begin occurring?

35

You may hold a belief, a concept in the subconscious mind, "I deserve to be punished because I did not do what I was told to do." Some authority figure could have told you that you deserved to be punished. You had been bad, you were wrong. The subconscious mind holds on to that belief and creates the fulfillment of that belief, even to the extent of disease and physical death.

There are those who consciously and truly desire a healing and say, "Oh, how I wish I could be healed!"

Yet the subconscious mind is stating, "No, you deserve punishment. You deserve pain because you did something wrong." And the wrong may be related to the beliefs of the conscious mind at that time. In this instance, there will not come a healing.

There needs to come a blending, an understanding of what is in the conscious mind and what is in the subconscious mind. The desire for a healing needs to exist throughout the total being, or there will not be a permanent healing.

Yes, you can run off to one healer over here or another healer over there. A healer can work on you, directing energy to you. Then, you go away and the difficulty begins coming back. And you wonder what is going on with the body. You wonder why there is not a good healer!

If the cause is not healed, there will not be a permanent healing, in terms of the effect. But also understand, beloved friends, in the greater truth you are your own healer. Only you can heal you. That does not mean you cannot go forth and ask for assistance from ones in the non-physical or physical who understand how energies work. In truth, a healer never heals another person. A healer will assist the flow of energy, like recharging your batteries. But if you do not continue charging your own batteries, then the drainage of energy will continue occurring.

Disease is created when your own energy system becomes stagnated. If your chakras, meaning your energy points, become stagnated, their energy is not being replenished. It is as if there is a drain in the energy field. And this energy field is not creating a nourishing energy to the physical form. Depending on which chakra is blocked, not blocked one hundred percent, but blocked in terms of stagnation, part of the body will become diseased, will feel pain, will feel discomfort, and will be at dis-ease with its own self.

Your own electromagnetic energy field flows through the body creating a rejuvenation of the body. A lack or stagnation of that energy will create aging. It will create what you would call wrinkles in the face or pain in the joints. So many believe growing old in your body, or becoming old and decrepit, is a natural state. It is an unnatural state. But because you look all around you in your human world and see that everybody grows old, you believe aging must be natural.

How often do you allow your mind to compare yourself with others? That is giving away your power. And when you give away your power, depending on which attitude you are carrying which is giving away that power, your body will be affected in certain chakras or energy points. That energy begins draining from you. Your electromagnetic energy field becomes stagnated. It is then not rejuvenating that part of the body. It is not even rejuvenating your own emotional body. It is not rejuvenating your own mental body.

You are not someone else. You are your own unique individual God-self. And we use the word "God" in terms of the ancient meaning of this word, creative source. You are creative beings. It is true that some create more than others. It is also true that some create more pain than others. Some create more joy than others. Yet, you are all of the God essence because every one of you creates continuously. You do not always create what the mind, the conscious mind, would desire to create. But nonetheless, you are still creating.

Understanding this is of great importance. The subconscious mind has the same power to create as your conscious mind. Therefore, one can be running around searching for enlightenment, reading all of the latest books, even searching out all of the latest mediums, one can be searching for his or her own enlightenment on a conscious level, put everything into practice one believes he or she is supposed to do, and still wonder, "Why is my life the same? Why has it not changed? Why do I still have such difficulty with my family, relatives, friends, work, wife, husband, children?"

It is because the programming is still there in your subconscious mind, whatever that programming may be. We will speak later on how to search and come to an understanding of what is in the subconscious mind and what has been programmed there. We will speak about how to begin working with that part of yourself equally with the conscious mind and with your emotional feelings, and the expression of those emotional feelings.

The power of healing is equal for everyone. It is not only selected individuals who have an open doorway to the healing energies of the Universe. Every one of you has equal access to the universal healing energies.

Also, there is no disease that cannot and has not been healed. We understand that this statement is in contradiction to certain scientific theories from your medical profession, that there are some diseases which are terminal. If you believe thoughts like, "I cannot be healed. I am definitely going to die," then you will because you will fulfill your own prophecy which you have accepted as an absolute truth.

We are not stating here to negate or to ignore medical treatment when you choose it as an aid, but believing that only medical treatment will heal you or cure you is not of truth. Medical treatment can be utilized as a tool, even in bringing the understanding of what difficulty exists, but the ultimate healer is yourself. The ultimate decision to be healed lies within yourself. Only you can stand in the way of yourself.

Do you want to be healed? Truly, do you want to be healed? Is there a part of you that is using the disease for another reason which is not of a positive nature? Is there a part of you using the disease, or even mental emotional depression, to try to gain the attention of another or others? Is there a part of you using the disease in terms of revenge? Only you can answer those questions. You can answer those questions when you make a choice to be honest with yourself, with your feelings, and with your innermost desires.

Is there a part of you that experienced a trauma as a child, where as a child you believed someone did something wrong to you, someone hurt you and therefore you are going to get back at that person? It is not that you would hold this in your conscious mind, necessarily, but that the subconscious mind would hold on to a belief that you will get even. You will create something where you have to be taken care of because you are tired of taking care of others. With that attitude, you were taking care of others because of a lack of self-esteem. Now, understand carefully the words we are using here in terms of taking care of others. We are not saying not to assist others, not to love others, or not to be there for others. We are saying not to carry the responsibility of others, because if you do, you will begin absorbing their energy. You will begin creating your own stagnation, your own depression, your own anger, your own rage, which you have hidden even from yourself.

The body never lies. The mind will often lie to itself and seek to deceive itself even in order to gain approval of the most popular thought of the time, meaning the mass conscious thought. It is important to understand the human energies and how they work. It is important to understand yourself as more than just a physical body. It is important to understand how your conscious and subconscious mind work. It is important to understand how your emotions work, particularly for the males of your society who are taught to suppress the emotional feelings, the emotional expression. Males are taught that emotional expression is a sign of weakness. They are taught that they must become the great intellectual. It is that concept and thought that created the denial of equality between man and woman, even though man and woman in totality are equal.

Deny the emotions you feel, deny the expression of what you feel, and your body will self-destruct. You will create cancer. But the cancer will be created in the particular part of the body which directly correlates with that particular emotion or attitude.

Cancer is a word that strikes fear in the minds of many. One can have a creation of cancer within their body and not be aware of it physically, not have it shown in the body physically. One can carry cancer of the mind, cancer of the emotions, or cancer of the spirit and not have it manifested within the physical. Within the physical, there are over two thousand forms of cancer, and more forms of cancer are continually being created. There are many more different levels of cancer in the mental and emotional bodies.

One can create cancer in their physical body, have the cancer cut out of the body, have different chemicals to fight the cancer within the body, and one may even be perceived they are now cancer-free. And in the physical that may be quite true. But it is not necessarily true in terms of the energy of cancer. One can have that cancer physically removed and still carry the energy of cancer. One can still have that cancer reappear again in the physical, or indeed, one can have it where the cancer never again in this particular lifetime returns to the physical, yet still carry the energy of cancer.

Cancer eats away at the body, the mind and the emotions. It can create holes within your energy field that can allow many different forms of energy that are not compatible with you to enter into your own energy field. The energy of cancer eats away at the feeling state and carries a tendency for a person to look at himself or herself as a failure, with hopelessness.

The energy of cancer is quite similar to a virus. Just as a virus enters into a body, it attacks the immune system, specifically weakened immune systems. There is more than simply the physical immune system. There is also the spiritual immune system, the mental immune system, and the emotional immune system. The energy of cancer can very easily attract the mass consciousness, mass fear, and mass anxiety into the mind and emotions.

The energy of cancer will increase before it subsides in your culture. One of the reasons is the continuing pollution of your planet, your bodies, your minds, and your emotions. Just as your physical body can carry many different forms of pollution and toxins, the mind and the emotions can also carry much pollution and toxins.

As your world becomes more compressed, as your world becomes more depressed, as your world becomes more filled with anxiety of wars and rumors of wars, as your world fills with more anxiety of new diseases and new viruses emerging daily in your physical plane, it becomes critically important to learn how to feel. And it is a learning process. Few are ever born totally aware of how to feel, just as an infant is not born knowing how to instantly speak a particular language, how to walk, or how to run. Do not assume that an infant is born knowing how to feel. What is of import is learning how to feel and not take it for granted. And it is not having an explosion of emotions and perceiving that is learning how to feel.

Many confuse truly feeling with simply expressing emotions. And many emotions that are expressed over and over and over again become a habit, a habitual expression of emotions. This has nothing to do with feelings. Learning how to feel is learning what is occurring in your mind, conscious and subconscious, what is occurring in your body, what is occurring in your environment. Learning to feel is to be aware of the energy that surrounds you, including the energy of thoughts, of thought forms, of what is preparing to manifest in your environment, what is preparing to manifest in your body, or what is preparing to manifest in your emotions, or your mind. Learning to feel can bring awareness to you if depression is going to be occurring, if there is going to be a pain occurring in the body, a difficulty occurring in the body. Learning to feel can prepare you for what is preparing to manifest in your own creation.

Are you one who suppresses feelings? This is not to confuse with suppressing emotions. Are you one that carries great empathy for others but

Good!

you have difficulty in allowing yourself to feel that empathy and then to express that feeling? Are you one that has a tendency to want to carry the energy of others? Are you one that carries deep seated anger, even unrecognized deep seated anger, and you are not quite sure how to allow yourself to feel that energy in order to positively release the energy? Do you have a tendency to bring energy into your body, into your mind, into your emotions over and over and over again without allowing for an outlet of that energy? If you are one that continues taking on energy without an outlet, it will begin eating away at your body, your mind, your emotions, and your spirit. Even what some may perceive as a positive gesture, meaning one carries great empathy for the condition of the world, and they take on themselves the pain and the suffering of the world, but they do not allow an outlet for it, they take on the energy without allowing an outlet, that energy, my friends, will eat away at the mind, the emotions, the body, the physical, and the spirit.

Not everyone will heal their physical bodies of cancer. Many will choose to leave the physical through physical cancer. Indeed, one can physically die from cancer and still take the cancer with them, mentally and emotionally. If the cancer is not healed in the non-physical state, it is oftentimes returned again to the physical, and again, creates cancer over and over and over again. There is never an escape, there is only resolvement.

There are many different levels of healing, and sometimes death is a healing. Sometimes ones create cancer so that they may create a much deeper search within themselves as to their own meaning in life, that they may search their own inner abilities and opportunities to heal. Some create cancer because they are oblivious to their environments. They are oblivious to what they have been doing to their mind, to their emotions, to their bodies for years and years and years. They have developed certain patterns that have become quite destructive, yet not fully recognized. Sometimes ones will create cancer to look at those patterns, heal those patterns, and heal the disease by whatever tools are available to them, whether it be Eastern medicine or Western medicine. Judge not one type of medicine over the other. They are both tools of healing.

If you create a disorder in the body, will you allow yourself to learn from it? Will you allow yourself to grow from that disorder? Will you allow yourself to truly understand, comprehend, and integrate that learning throughout your energetic system and truly allow for a healing? Which means, and this is important to understand, one can create a disorder in the body in order to learn, whatever it is one may need to learn, and one indeed can heal on many levels because of that disorder, but that healing may not manifest within the physical plane, meaning within the physical body. However, because one truly learned from it and created change in one's life, because one truly healed the mind and emotions, and truly healed whatever conflicts were there, that one does not carry the disorder with the self from the physical.

When the desire is strong enough to heal, there will be a healing, but that healing will not always be in the physical. Yes, the physical is important to many people, but the spiritual, mental and emotional healing is a much more powerful healing. That is the healing, my friends, that remains with you wherever you may journey through time.

When one comes to a deeper level of understanding of disease, not being at-ease with oneself, is when one comes to a greater understanding of how to heal the disease. By coming to understand the disease, to understand the pattern that created the disease, understand the mental thinking pattern, the emotional pattern, and also one's physical pattern, what one places into the body when one is not capable of transcending to positively release the energy, by coming to a deeper level of understanding of disease is when one comes to a greater understanding of how to heal the disease.

Whatever disease of the body, whatever part of you is not at-ease with your mind, whatever part of you is not at-ease with your emotions, was created by yourself. And that is why we state and we will continue to state, "Only you can heal you."

The healing energies of the Universe do not separate or play favoritism. The healing energies of the Universe do not choose, "This one will be healed, this one will not be healed."

Many believe in a god outside of themselves, in a male authority figure somewhere out there who remains hidden and says, "I will heal this one, I will not heal that one."

Cease placing power outside of yourself. When you do that, you allow your own energy to be drained, you allow fearing. Fear is created because you have placed power outside of yourself. If you were to put no power outside of yourself, you would fear nothing. Ponder that thought, my friends.

If you make a decision not to place power outside of yourself, there would be nothing to fear. And we well understand the attitudes and the thoughts in the mind that say, "It is much easier said than done."

Is it? Or is that simply a convenient thought, so one will then not work upon it? Truly ponder this statement. How often do you simply choose a convenient statement, when in truth you are denying your own existence, you are denying your own power?

Many say, "I will believe it when I see it."

We say, "You will see it when you believe it!" Because what you believe, you experience. Believe in yourself. Believe that you have the power to heal, and then you will be healed. Because what you are doing in making that statement is reclaiming your power, reclaiming your identity, reclaiming your own love for yourself. And when you reclaim that love for yourself, then you have the ability to understand what judgment is. Those who do not love, do not understand judgment.

So many are programmed to judge. They are not even aware they are judging. But when one begins entering into that energy of self-loving, one comes to understand judgment, see judgment, and release judgment.

Many say that they do not judge, yet they truly do not know themselves. When we use the word "judgment" we are referring to self-judgment, which is also self-denial.

By allowing yourself to love yourself, you are coming to understand every part of yourself, the part of yourself that seeks the Light and the part of yourself that exists in a lesser light. Many who seek a pathway to enlightenment will only seek to look at what is called enlightenment, but what they are doing is negating different parts of themselves which have been created in a lesser light. They are negating their own self-creation. While many are focusing their conscious minds only on enlightenment, they can still be in separation, denial, and negation of their own selves.

It is important to understand this concept and the concept of separation. One can be searching to such a degree, such an extent, for one's own enlightenment, while negating another part of oneself, which is not searching for enlightenment. To bring a greater understanding of this concept, one can use the example of how one can create a disease in a particular part of the body, but work on strengthening another part of the body, pretending the disease does not exist in that other part of the body. That is not taking into account the whole body, the oneness of all that exists. The same applies when one chooses a pathway of searching for enlightenment. Searching for enlightenment is in truth allowing oneself to search *all* parts of the self so that nothing will become hidden. If just the conscious mind searches for enlightenment, without working or searching within the subconscious mind, or the emotions, then in the greater truth, that is not a pathway towards enlightenment, but is a pathway of negation and escapism.

Again, it is important to understand this concept because the denial of understanding this particular concept is one of the key factors why many do not create their own healing in totality.

Envision yourself as if you are standing in the center of a field, and directly in front of you is a trail, a pathway. And you believe that only that one pathway leads to enlightenment. Yet all around you are trails. There are many pathways leading out in different directions, going different ways. To hold the belief that only the one pathway is the way to find enlightenment is making a statement on another level. You are denying and escaping what the other pathways have to offer, which are also of enlightenment, even though the conscious mind at this point and time may not be aware that all the pathways lead to enlightenment.

To allow yourself to become totally enlightened is to see yourself as part of the whole. Envision yourself as if you are a single cell of a body, and that body is made of billions upon billions of cells. You as a single cell maintain your own individuality, your own uniqueness, and your own purpose. Yet the greater purpose is not separated from the whole body which encompasses the billions upon billions of cells. And if one part of that body feels pain, feels a disease, all of the cells offer assistance in the healing of that part of the body which is in pain.

And this is why many souls are coming to the Earth plane to speak a message of light, to speak a message of love, and to speak a message of enlightenment. This is because part of the body is hurting. And part of that body, in this particular instance, is called your world. Many cells, many beings of light, are coming here to assist in the healing, not to do it for you, but to assist in the healing.

You as an individual person may desire to heal a particular part of your own body. You can do so by becoming aware of the whole body, which means by becoming aware of your own emotions, becoming aware of your attitudes, and of your thoughts, conscious and subconscious. You can work on the whole, but not just from the point of view of your conscious mind, making a statement such as, "I want to be healed, therefore I will find this pathway to enlightenment and I will only be on this one narrow pathway and forget all else."

In this manner would you become enlightened? Indeed not. You would become more frustrated. You may even agitate the disease, to where the disease would become more painful.

There is no separation in all that exists. Unite the oneness of yourself. Allow yourself to unite your conscious mind, your subconscious mind, and your emotional body with your own soul essence, with your own inner light, and allow that inner light to spread throughout the totality of your body, meaning, the totality of your consciousness, and the totality of your subconscious. And healing will begin occurring.

Understand that the majority, not all, but the majority of the illnesses and diseases, whether they be physical, mental, or emotional in terms of the pain you feel, began in your childhood. How many of you remember your childhood? If there are particular time frames in your childhood which have been blocked out and you do not remember, usually the reason is because there was a trauma that occurred then. It does not necessarily have to have been a physical trauma. It could have been a mental or an emotional trauma. It could have been that a belief which was contrary to your inner knowing was absorbed into your energy field. And that belief began eating away at you.

Even though the conscious mind as a child may have pushed the belief away, and may have chosen to forget it ever existed, that belief and energy which was contrary to your own inner energy, could have begun eating at you and eventually turned into a disease, into a depression, into fear, anger, or rage.

As we stated earlier in this message, we will discuss how to come to know what is in your subconscious mind. At this time, allow yourself to enter into a meditative state, which simply means to quiet the mind.

Now, for those of you who believe it is difficult to sit still because you are active and energetic, who believe it is difficult for you to meditate, would benefit by going to nature to meditate. Go to where there is movement of water, whether that movement be a creek, a river, or even a beach, where the water moves up on the beach. That movement of water will assist you in quieting the mind.

When you have entered into a state of meditation, visualize yourself as a child. It is important not to try to work on it to where it has to be perfect, where you have to find this perfect vision of what you looked like physically as a child. Simply allow this vision to begin emerging of yourself as a child. Allow that vision to come forth with an impression of what you looked like as a child.

When you have done this, speak to the child. First, tell this child that the child does not deserve punishment. Speak to this child and tell the child that he or she is worthy of being loved unconditionally. Speak to this child and tell this child that he or she never has to prove himself or herself at any time to anyone. Then, begin building a bond between you, the adult, and you, the child. Verbally speak this message in this vision. Begin asking the child what the child thinks of you as an adult. Does that child trust you as an adult? Work with the belief system of this child.

Understand, when you create this vision, you are creating a link of energy between the conscious and subconscious mind. You are beginning to unite and heal the attitudes, thoughts, and programming that you are bad, that you deserve punishment. It is important to understand that what the mind believes, it will experience.

You will see it when you believe it. The question is—what do you want to see?

Do you want to see prosperity, laughter, joy, companionship, or do you want to see negation, separation, pain, disease, anger, or depression? What do you believe you are worthy of? And regarding the search for your own healing, your own enlightenment, allow yourself to search all parts of yourself, not just one part. Do you know that every cell of your body carries a consciousness, and that consciousness is programmed to the belief system you have absorbed and accepted even as a child? And when a child holds a belief that the child does not even deserve to live, that the child does not deserve to be loved, the mind is programming the cellular structure of the body with that belief, with that consciousness.

You will experience what you believe even if that belief is an old belief. If it has not been released and healed, then the belief is still there and it is still working on your body. When you come to love yourself, you will truly understand the concept of judgment. Judgment comes from fear and separation. When you allow yourself to love yourself you will come to see what needs to be healed. But negate self loving, and you will not know what is in need of healing. You can go to all the healers in your world and there will not be a permanent healing. A temporary energizing from time to time, yes.

Only you can heal you. Understand this statement well. We are not saying you are all alone in your healing. The creative God-source, which is of all lovingness and knowingness, will assist any who request assistance and are willing to receive assistance. The key here is that the creative God-source will not do it for you, but will assist you as you ask and are willing to receive. The willingness to receive comes from searching your own self-respect, your own commitment to yourself and to the whole.

First, choose what you want. Then, search for the intent of what you want. Is the intent based upon escapism? Is the intent based upon fear? Is the intent based upon judgment? Or is the intent based upon the desire of loving the self unconditionally?

Intent is the building block of the outcome. Choose what you want. Search your intent of why you want it. Then, become totally committed to creating it. There is no one who has power over you.

There is no one who has authority who can come and say that you do not deserve it. We well understand that this thought exists in many minds, but it only exists in the minds because those minds have given their power away. Become committed to yourself because you are worth it, because you are a unique beautiful being who is seeking the understanding of a pureness of light. You are seeking the understanding that you deserve an existence of peace, joy, and perfect health, meaning that the body is functioning in totality, that the body is functioning in equal vibration with the soul. The soul carries its own inner vibration, its own inner frequency of the electromagnetic energy field. If the human consciousness and human emotions are out of sync with that inner frequency, then there is going to be a disturbance in the human energy system.

The simple key is to come to that state of awareness that you are worthy of being loved unconditionally, of coming to that point of awareness that you do not deserve punishment, of bringing your mind and your emotions back into harmony with the soul vibration.

We understand that there are certain teachings and concepts that purport that some have created a disease to fulfill karma. However, negative karma only exists when unconditional loving does not. Hold on to the belief that you have to have the disease to fulfill karma, and you will hold on to that disease. But there is no universal law which dictates you must do that. That is your own choosing.

What do you want, my friends? And what do you believe you deserve? Believe simply in the doctrine of your world which has forgotten how to live, you will forget how to live and you will only work on survival. Come to remember your heritage, your spiritual heritage. Come to remember your own unlimited power. Come to remember that you are an equal soul. Come to remember that you are an enlightened master, that you simply forgot for awhile, but now you are coming to remember again and you will have the power to heal.

You will have the power to heal whatever part of yourself has been in a state of disease. And as you heal yourself, you begin working with the whole and assisting the healing of your mother, Mother Earth, which supplies the nutrients of life for your physical bodies.

As the world so dictates, "I will believe it when I see it," the Universe of light, of love, of compassion says, "You will see it when you believe it."

Now, what do you choose to believe? That will be your experience in this incarnation. The choice is always yours. The power of healing is there for the asking. Ask for it through the wholeness, allowing yourself to be united with the-oneness-of-all-there-is, and finally end separation. Allow yourself to join in the family of healers in the healing of your Mother Earth. Become one. Become one with what is called the-oneness–of-all-there-is and allow yourself to end separation.

5

The God of Life

Good day to those who truly desire an understanding of truth, not a single truth, but a multi-dimensional truth, a truth which will be known, felt, and recognized on the Earth plane. So much has been spoken of the New Age, the new government, and those who are trying to create a new religion to fulfill the needs of the New Age.

We will speak of what God is. We will speak of the creative force of the God-nature. We will speak of what space is, inner space, outer space, and space in general.

Indeed, some would call us a god from outer space! Outer space? Does the word "space" simply mean spaciousness? The word "space" implies the ability to create within a space. Perceive it as a room which allows you an area in which to create. But also understand that when the mind holds thoughts of limitation such as, "Where is the outline in space? Where are the boundaries of space?" the mind is limiting your creativity.

Where is the limitation of space? It does not exist. Neither is there a limitation of your creativity, your own godship, or your own mastership.

Indeed, we are a god. But so are you a god! The only difference between you being a god and us being a god, is that we have not forgotten what it is like to be a god. We have not forgotten what it is like to be a master. A master is simply one who carries knowledge and wisdom combined with simplicity and unconditional lovingness. Knowledge and wisdom without lovingness is not knowledge and wisdom.

Many have pondered, "Who is this called Jonah?"

Why have we come to your Earth? Indeed, we have chosen the label "Jonah" because of its vibratory level. Each name carries a vibratory level. The word "Jonah" carries two aspects. One aspect is the double-edged sword. It cuts two ways: it cuts through the ego, and it cuts through the maze to allow knowledge and wisdom to be understood in your Earth plane. It also represents the dove, which represents freedom.

We have been known upon your Earth plane in prior times as the "Teacher of Righteousness." Let it be known we have come again as the teacher of freedom, to teach and bring an understanding of freedom, an understanding of what true joy is. We have come to teach that true joy can be accomplished. It can be achieved without great difficulty.

We have come again to your Earth plane because in this day and age you have not understood the message we brought to you two thousand years ago. Indeed, there are those you call historians who do not understand history. There are those who seek to study ancient documents about our existence. But understand that those who wrote the documents were not pleased about our message. Therefore, we chose again to come forth to the Earth plane to speak for ourselves, and not to have historians who do not understand history speak for us. We desire no one to take responsibility for us. We have come and will remain until the New Age, the philosophy of God, and the understanding of the God-nature within each of you is understood on Earth. Then, we will return to our home.

Our home is a universe beyond yours. Your scientists have not yet discovered our universe, nor will they because of the acceptance of limitation. Understand, universes exist within universes within universes within universes. It is not so much a travel of time from where we exist, but a travel of recognition. When ones truly come to understand their own recognition, their own God essence, our universe is simply but a thought away.

We come from a universe created from light, sound, and color. In our universe, communication is within musical notes. There are no secrets where we come from. Each entity is simply known by the vibration of the musical notes, the musical tones. Each is understood and accepted as a friend of the heart. There are no enemies, adversaries, devils, or satans, which your world is consumed with fear that they exist.

The thought projection of mankind has created a devil. Thought projection has created what religious terminologies call Satan. Satan represents the denial of the God essence within each one. Satan represents the denial of truth, your inner truth, not someone else's truth. Whether one is physical or non-physical, the denial is of your own inner truth. We are not speaking about what has been programmed into your mind, what you think the truth is. We are referring to you as a soul, as an eternal being of light, of truth, and of simplicity. When you deny this, this denial is the satanic attitude. Satan simply means you missed the mark. You are not understanding your own God-nature. You are seeking to place God outside of yourself. And to what avail? To please the programming of the mind?

Is it not time for you to stop playing games? Indeed, understand that many gods from many universes have come to your Earth to assist, to bring an understanding of light, of the true Christed-consciousness which is eternal, which has always been and which will always be. But when we use the word "Christed-consciousness" we are not talking about organized Christianity. We are referring to a concept within you that exists but has been so buried and hidden within each of you, as a soul, hidden by the mind. We are speaking about a concept which society has programmed to hide within its religious natures of fear, fear of a god who would burn his children.

The only god who exists who would burn his children is a manmade god. The Universe does not punish. We cannot force you to believe it. We will not even try. We will only make the statement. Understand, those who have eyes will see. Those who have ears will hear. We have not come to your Earth to create a following. We have not come to your Earth to create a worshipping. We have come to your Earth to bring peace, to teach peace. Those who choose to listen will indeed live in peace.

We have not come to your world to create confusion, nor to judge or condemn. But as an old saying of your English language goes, we will "call a spade a spade." And simply speaking of what is occurring is not judgment.

It is important to understand that what has been occurring in your world cannot continue or you will destroy your planet. Many gods of the Universe are well aware of this. That is why many masters have come to bring an enlightenment to your society. The Earth is an entity, and you cannot trespass on the free-will choice of another entity. To state it in other terms, you cannot continue trying to destroy the Earth through greed.

As we have spoken to you before, the year of the comet was the beginning of great changes, the beginning of drought, the beginning of earthquakes, and the beginning of understanding that you have a decision to make. The decision must be yours. It cannot be another's decision. So, what will you choose? Pain or true joy?

We understand there are many in your society who say, "But it is such a simple answer to choose between pain or joy."

Many people will say that there are many other alternatives in between. Indeed not. You have created thought forms which are still in existence in your world which have not been recognized, which have not changed, and which will create much pain. What we are here to teach is that the Universe is simple. Indeed it is. The choice is simple. Pain or true joy? Lovingness or hatred? Compassion or judgment? They are different words which ask the same thing.

It is easy for many to judge when they do not understand. It is easy to fear when they do not understand.

It does not require a belief for the New Age to come about. It simply is. What society calls the New Age movement is not coming about simply because a group of individuals desire it. Yes, it is partly coming about because of the change in the human consciousness. But that is not the totality.

The entity called Earth is also desiring the New Age of thought. The New Age is a new level of consciousness, a new level of thought, a greater reality of peace. Many of you sit in your small boxes you call homes and allow your minds to become burdened with daily activities, relationships, work, problems with the children, problems with the neighbor, even problems with the automobile! When you have a problem with your automobile it is simply a reflection of a problem you are having with your life. Not all want to hear this, but it is still the truth.

Every difficulty you carry is a direct reflection of your state of mind. How long have you been dwelling on negative thoughts, with fears of a certain problem, and indeed, the problem surfaces? You are confronted with the problem. You are confronted with your own creation.

The word "God" simply means creative force. The Earth has a creative force. You will see it from time to time in your earthquakes, volcanoes, hurricanes, droughts, and tornados. So, what will you do about it?

As we have spoken in other messages, there have been, and are, masters and gods. Masters and gods are beings who can create the purity of truth so that unconditional loving, unconditional acceptance will be known. But be assured they will not force change upon you.

Understand that we are not here to force ourselves upon you. We are here to teach, and through bringing a teaching and enlightenment to your world, we assist you in finding your own God-force. No one will do it for you. And anyone who states he or she will do it for you is not of truth.

Indeed, you will be assisted to whatever degree is necessary. You will be guided to whatever degree is necessary. You will never be forced by truth. We well understand that there is great confusion in your world. And because of the confusion, many are looking for a complicated method of survival.

To survive what? Life? Life is eternal. So many human minds are eagerly looking for survival of the human form, the human body, their human existence after physical death. But we have spoken of this physical death before.

Understand, the truth is simple. There is a key we will give you. It is a simple key, and one need not be a scholar to understand it: one cannot understand truth until one makes the decision to love. This is a simple truth. How many are willing to live it? So many live in the confusion of the mind. They cannot understand truth. They cannot understand their God-nature. They cannot listen to their inner voice. They cannot channel their Higher-self. They cannot because they choose not to love.

When you choose to love you can come into an attunement with your inner self. There need not be the difficulties of survival. Many complain constantly, "Why the trauma? Why the trials? Why the test? Why the difficulties of life?"

A simple answer—because you do not love yourself.

We well know there are going to be those who do not believe the statement because they are still carrying the attitude that they are being punished by some outside force. The only force which can create a disturbance in your life, outside of yourself, can only do it when you do not love yourself, when you do not claim responsibility for yourself as a god.

Life and the pursuit of happiness, the pursuit of freedom, are principles which your founding fathers established in the constitution of the United States of America. Understand, many of the founding fathers were in contact with gods from other universes. Well, so much for religion!

Religion is a concept. Religion is a philosophy. Religion is an idea brought about by mankind to try to create a focus for mankind. But what direction or focus will you choose? A focus outside of yourself, or a focus inside of yourself? Will you choose to place all of your trust in a god outside of yourself whom you have not even met? Will you choose to look to a savior some call the Son of God to wipe away all of your sins, to assist in removing your guilt?

Guilt is an energy, an energy of the inability to forgive yourself because you believe you have transgressed a law, whether the law be in truth or falsehood. Religion is an invention of mankind.

Understand, we have not come to your Earth to condemn religion. We have not come to your Earth to condemn the human mind. We have not come to your Earth to condemn the pain in which you continue to live. We have come to your Earth again to bring a teaching, a teaching which will raise your consciousness, a teaching which will bring enlightenment, a teaching which will bring freedom and the knowledge that you do not need to follow a god. You do not need to follow a master. You do not need to follow a religion. You do not need to follow an organization.

We have come forth to bring a teaching of simplicity to the human mind so that you will choose to stop living in pain. Indeed, there are many changes which will come to your Earth, changes in the masses of water, the masses of land, and changes in the human consciousness. They will come as a direct result of the percentages who choose to make a decision to continue living in the negation of life, in a denial of life.

We, the Jonah, have come again to your Earth because we love you, as you would call yourselves the human race, unconditionally. And we love the entity called Earth unconditionally. The Earth has asked us to return again. Many of the souls of light have asked us to return again, but not to save you. There is no savior. But indeed, there is enlightenment. You may save your own self from pain, whether it be relationships, finances, disease, or whatever it may be.

Understand that by allowing your human consciousness to become a part of your inner God-self, your inner Christ-self, by becoming unified within your own beingness, then, and only then, will the healing occur of the pain and the trauma, whatever the magnitude may be.

My friends, there is no savior coming to save you. We understand this statement may create anger for those who have lived their lives looking for someone to save them, looking for a god to take care of them. You are responsible for all you think, all you do, and all you create. And we will repeat this again, and again, and again. You are responsible for you.

The God-force of the Universe loves you unconditionally. The Christ-force loves you unconditionally. But it is not the responsibility of that force to carry your responsibility. Indeed, it is our responsibility to come and to teach a message of freedom. And it is not one singular message. There are multiple messages of freedom. Many will say, "Well, it is easy for this one to say that it is easy to love oneself unconditionally."

Twice we have been in human form. We understand how difficult you believe it is to love yourself unconditionally. This is the same degree of difficulty regarding the denial of yourself. It is so easy for the human mind to make the statements, "It is difficult for one to love oneself. It is difficult for one to live in true joy."

Why is it not simple for you to say that you will live a life of true joy?

Say this daily, hourly, by the minute, if you need to. What is stopping you? Is it that your human programming makes you feel that you must live a life of pain in order to grow? Indeed, pain does create growth. It does. But so does true joy. Which will you accept? Pain? Joy? Joy or pain?

What you desire out of lovingness is yours when you allow yourself to receive it. As we said before, we were here in a prior time as the "Teacher of Righteousness." The word "righteousness" meant right thought for you, not for the masses, but the right thought for you. In other words, it was a teaching of choosing a positive thought for you, a positive life for you, a positive recognition of your own God-force. We were not accepted by traditional religion during that age, nor by government. Nor again are we accepted by traditional religion!

Many warn, "Do not talk to spirits!" Well, what are you if you are not a soul, if you are not a spirit? Familiar spirits is a term many utilize to create fear. "Do not converse with the familiar spirits," so says the scripture in your ancient book called the Bible. Most of that book is not as ancient as you think. Much of it has been rewritten in accordance to the pleasing of the ego. But so be it.

The original term "familiar spirits" was the true meaning of what we would categorize as earthbound spirits, spirits who have not ascended, spirits who have not released their negativity which bound them to the world mind. The true meaning of the scripture is: do not try to seek knowledge from an entity who has not yet ascended, a familiar spirit to the world mind which is of pain, fear, and negation of life.

We in the non-physical state have come to assist in the healing of the heart and the healing of the mind. The human mind has asked for assistance. The Earth entity has asked for assistance. And we have come to offer it, not to force it. The God-force of the Universe, of the Christed-consciousness, does not judge. Judgment is a condition of the human mind to establish guilt and fear to create a following, a following toward fulfilling the human ego.

It is time to awaken! It is time for you to begin speaking truth. It is not time for you to fall asleep again and forget who you are. It is time to awaken the Christed-consciousness within you.

The degree of negativity, of ones seeking to remain in negativity, is the same degree of the Earth changes which will occur. The Earth's physical changes of land mass, water mass, and weather, which you would call weather patterns, the jet stream patterns, is not a punishment. It is a cleansing. Those of you who choose to fear this cleansing will be affected by the cleansing. Those of you who choose to live in the faith of your own God-self, not a faith in another being, not faith in us, not faith in the Christ, but a faith in yourself as a totality of the God, of the Christ, of the creative force, to that degree you will learn.

You need not run about in fear, seeking a place to hide because of the many changes. Christianity calls it tribulation. We call it a cleansing, and not because there is a singular god, angry and vengeful, who seeks to punish. The entity called Earth desires to create a cleansing to allow the growth, the evolutionary process of the human development of enlightenment, to continue to occur.

Those who will seek to hide out of fear are those who will not find a place to hide. Live not in fear of the changes coming to your Earth. Rejoice in the New Age, new thought, and higher state of consciousness. Every two thousand years there is a new age. Jesus, whose true name was Jeshua, came to speak of the New Age, the Piscean age, the age you have been living in for two thousand years, which some would now call the Old Age. Jesus came to prepare the human consciousness for the new age of that particular time, two thousand years ago.

And who fought Jesus but religion and government? The old saying goes, "History repeats itself." Souls do not need to repeat themselves. Indeed, souls who seek not the Light or the Christed-consciousness will fight because of fear. They will fight the arrival of the New Age, just as they did two thousand years ago.

They called Jesus a liar, a false prophet. Both the religion of that time and the governments condemned him. To a greater degree religion condemned him because it feared losing control over the mind of the masses which it controlled to satisfy its ego.

Judge not religion, but love it unconditionally. Love it because it is creating an opposite polarity to create growth, advancement, and achievement. Love government unconditionally because it is creating growth and movement. To love a negative energy does not mean to participate in the negative energy. Understand that if you judge the negative energy you will only increase its power. Loving a negative energy decreases its power and influence over you. Understand this well. There cannot be judgment.

We have never made a claim that we have come to please the mind of mankind. We never will. But we have come to bring a teaching to mankind.

The return of Jonah is present. We have come again, not to judge or condemn, but to bring an enlightenment to the human consciousness. Those who have eyes will see. Those who have ears will hear. Those who do not, will not. Those who now choose not to live by the light of the Christed-consciousness, in time will come to do so, whether it be in this incarnation or after ten thousand incarnations. It is a process of life, a growth of life.

Force truth on no one. Force your beliefs on no one. Live your truth, your inner truth, and your inner God-self. We have come to teach the masses. And indeed, we will. When this has been completed, we will return home. Your job is to teach the Light and the Truth. A teacher is a teacher when that person lives his or her own teaching. Indeed, we love all of you unconditionally.

6

Power of the Mind

depression

To understand the power of the mind and how it is utilized, one must first realize that there cannot be what is called an absolute. The existence of an absolute would remove what is called free-will choice. Therefore, there cannot be an absolute in all that exists.

Our purpose is to guide and assist you in becoming your own teacher and to assist your mind in listening and following your truth, not part of a truth of another. Every soul carries its own truth, its own core essence, its own core beingness, and its own individuality.

Many are taught in this society to look at another's truth, to look at what another is doing spiritually, and to go follow the other because of the results you see in the other. You begin following the other only to find pain, to find that the other's manifestations are not your manifestations. When you deny in your mind the truth of your heart, depression occurs. Whenever you are in a state of depression it is a sign that you are not living and following your own inner truth. This may be due to the programming of the mind, conscious or subconscious. Indeed, the mind is a creative powerful tool.

It is important to understand that the mind is not the brain, which is a physical organ. The mind is an energy field which sits on top of the head. It is an energy field which is of an electromagnetic energy essence. The mind is a transmitter and receiver of thought forms.

Thought is a condensed form of energy, universal energy, creative energy, the energy the Universe is made of. Perceive that energy as if it were a virgin energy and you would take that energy and convert it into thought, a thought form, a thought energy. The mechanism you utilize in creating that thought determines the type of energy that will be utilized in manifestation. The type of energy means either converting it into a positive energy, a negative energy, or even a neutral energy.

Within this school you call Earth, thought forms manifest into physical matter. We have often taught that what you believe is what you become. What you experience throughout life is based directly upon your own belief system, which consists of a combination of many thought forms which have entered the mind, consciously and subconsciously.

The mind sends forth thought forms to the brain structure that move electrolyte currents which then program every cell of the body. When the mind begins changing, the total cellular and molecular structure of the body also begins changing. When a cellular structure has been programmed from negative thought forms, painful thought forms, that energy begins absorbing, building, and creating toxins within the physical body. If enough toxins continually build and are not released within the physical structure, disease will occur. And indeed, your society well knows what disease is—that is when the body begins self-destruction. What occurs in the body, the physical body, is the last manifestation of the origination of that thought form.

To begin changing the energy of the mind is called taking total and complete responsibility. When the mind is not taking responsibility for itself, it taps into a mass consciousness, or what is called a world consciousness, where every thought that has ever been thought on this planet is still alive. It is still there. It is within this mass consciousness, when a mind is not taking responsibility for itself, that it begins drifting. The mind becomes attached to that mass consciousness, and then the mind begins to become programmed by those thoughts in the mass consciousness.

Recognize this when some of you are daydreaming, and you perceive some horrible thought that simply comes into the mind, and you wonder,

"Where did that come from?" It came from the mass consciousness, and it is called negation. You are responsible for you in totality. To allow the mass consciousness to control the mind, the mind will then create the environment to experience those thoughts physically. What you believe you become.

What will you allow in the mind? Every time you see, feel, and hear these negative thought forms entering into the mind, you have a choice to accept them, experiment with them, or to send them away, to begin shifting the electromagnetic energy field of the mind to simply allow positive energy, positive thoughts, to enter into the mind field that would begin cleansing the cellular structure of the body. And this process can heal any disease in existence in the Earth plane.

It is not just the brain which carries memories of the human organism, it is the total cellular structure which carries memory. This is why often times even a scarring on the emotional body which occurred many life-times ago, and which has not yet been healed, can be experienced when you come forth to incarnate again. You can still have pain in that location of the body where the pain was originally created. This is because the energy essence of the scarring on the emotional body is brought in from the memory of the mind essence and programs every cell of the body.

This is why from time to time you may find infants coming into the physical whose souls have been carrying karma, or what could be labeled as emotional scars which were not healed, which were not resolved in prior times. And you may find that there are difficulties within that body physically. This is because the mind energy is programming every cell of the body to change the mind to create a healing of the mind.

You may all notice when this occurs within yourselves. The physical body also goes through a shift. It goes through a cellular molecular structure shift. Sometimes you may feel nauseated. You may feel as if the body is changing, stretching. You will feel that the body is heavier or lighter at different times. Do you know this?

At-ease and dis-ease are concepts one needs to understand. When the mind is not in harmony with the heart essence, or the soul essence, dis-ease is created; ill-at-ease in the mind or dis-ease within the physical body structure begins.

There is not one disease which cannot be healed in the physical body. But indeed, there are many who believe that there are diseases which cannot be healed in the physical body. And those who carry that belief will not create healing in their body. The only limitation that exists is that to which you give power and credit.

Life is simple. But society's programming of the mind creates such hardships and difficulties in understanding the simplicity of life. Indeed, we could speak simply in one sentence, "Love yourself unconditionally," and that could cover the entirety of our message to you. But in simply stating this, many will not understand because of the many different levels of consciousness and the way the mind is taught to perceive and receive information. And this is neither right, wrong, good, or bad. Every one of you is different. You are different in your own method of creating. You are different in your own method of perceiving. You are different in your own manner of how you choose to be serious, fearful, joyous, and complex.

The power of the mind can create a universe. The power of the mind can move mountains. The power of the mind can create walking on water, walking through walls. The power of the mind can create disease and pain and separation, based on choice within its own belief structure. There are many minds and many human forms on many life systems, or what you would term planetary systems, throughout your universes.

The human minds on the Earth plane use approximately ten percent of their mind because your world teaches people to fear. The energy of fear blocks your development and your spiritual growth. Fear can be conscious or subconscious. Do you remember back in your own childhood when someone may have said to you that you were stupid and you believed it?

EMDR - desensitize

Or they said to you that you were bad, or that you were guilty, and you believed it?

That belief will always be there until that belief system is removed. That belief system can be covered over by the conscious mind with much pretending that it no longer exists, until you begin looking at your life, of what you have created, and you wonder why there are painful events occurring. You may state consciously that you cannot remember such an event in your childhood. How many can remember many events that lasted only thirty seconds in their childhood? However, just because the conscious mind cannot remember does not mean it is not there.

When the subconscious mind, the conscious mind, and the soul mind unite as one in harmony and togetherness, that is the sign that you are a master of your own reality. You know exactly at all times the totality of your beingness and what you are creating. We utilize the term "master of your own reality" when you know in totality what you are creating, when you are creating it, and how you are creating it.

The majority in your culture each day spend their time making decisions with the mind, calculating those decisions on beliefs, beliefs which are not necessarily theirs, but beliefs which have been accepted because they were beliefs of others. They begin using those beliefs within their mind field. And they begin creating a reality which slowly builds pain. Pressure begins building. Intensity begins building. And the body begins getting tighter and tighter and tighter. They begin having headaches, backaches, and leg aches. And they wonder what is going on.

Your society teaches to fix the effect and not the cause, because fixing the cause would mean to go inside and take a look. And many are fearful of truly going inside, fearful of what they might find, that they might find a being so filled with power, light, laughter and joy that they perceive they could not handle it!

Or there is the fear that they may go inside and find something dark and evil. Such a word "evil"! We do not see evil in your universe. We only see what is called light and some that is of a lesser light. What is of a lesser light is simply that which is seeking to understand and to grow in a different way. It is not a matter of good or bad, right or wrong. It is simply a matter of opposite polarities.

The power of the mind is used every second of your existence. Yet, how many times do you allow a counter check as to what has been entered into the mind? Everything you experience, see, hear, and feel is recorded within the mind energy constantly. Whatever you speak is the vibration of the energy which has been absorbed into the mind. Sometimes the mind does not take responsibility for what it allows into it. The mind will then begin absorbing energy from the mass consciousness. The mass consciousness is a collective consciousness of thought which often times can be quite negative. That collective consciousness can begin entering into the mind energy, the mind field, and create destructive forces.

To recognize this for yourself, ask yourself the question—how often have you been simply sitting minding your own business and a thought enters into the mind, and you begin to wonder where the thought came from? There are many different places the thought could have come from. The thought could have come from the mass consciousness, the mass energy, or the collective consciousness. Some would label it the collective unconscious! You can be picking up on a thought sent to you from another, or you can be thinking a thought which you have already received and buried in the subconscious of the mind which is coming forth to the conscious.

The mind is a transmitter and a receiver, much like your radio signals. The mouth is the speaker. The ears are the receiver, in terms of physical form, not just energy form.

One can speak and one can hear without using their physical ears or their physical mouth. But that is another story!

Indeed, the mind needs to be understood regarding its power and its ability. Nothing is impossible unless you believe in that impossibility. Recognize even how many times you have stated that you wish you could do this, you wish you could be that, and you wish you could have this. Truly look at the word "wish," which is something you desire but don't think you can have because you are not totally giving yourself the power and the credit of your own God-self that you deserve it.

Think of the energy of self-worth. Ask yourself the questions, and be honest with your own answers: What are you worth? What are you worth receiving? And what are you worth being?

Only you can answer those questions for yourself. Your beliefs regarding those answers are the outcome of your future. Your future is made up of what you think of yourself at this moment regarding your experiences and choices in those experiences.

As we said earlier, what you believe you become. What you think of yourself is what you will experience. And you will attract ones to you who will also think about you the way you think of yourself. They will not always talk about it. But they will perceive it. They will feel it. How many times have you asked why you cannot attract friends, mates, lovers, or relatives who simply accept you as you are, love you as you are? How many have held within their mind the thought, "If I were simply accepted as I am, how much stress would that remove from my life?"

Indeed, to achieve that desire, to have ones around who accept you as you are, you need to accept yourself as you are and to grow with that acceptance. You live in a society, in a culture, which teaches that the answers are always "out there," wherever "out there" happens to be. The power is always "out there." When we use the words "culture" or "society" we are not simply speaking of the country we are presently in, the one you call America, but rather the world culture, the world society as a whole.

"There is always something or someone 'out there' who can punish me, who can hurt me, who can depress me or sadden me."

There is nothing "out there." You are an individual god connected to the universal God essence because there is no separation. All answers, all truths lie within you.

You can never change something "out there" until it is already changed "in here." "In here" means yourself, regardless of the scope of what you desire to change. This is a concept we will share with you over and over again. You are the basis and the key to understanding your universal power and truth. And we well recognize that many of you have already heard the statement, "Do not place power outside of yourself."

But a philosophy is only a philosophy until it is lived, then it becomes a reality. There are many philosophies in the Universe. There are many philosophies in your human cultures. There are many different philosophies with every one who reads this material, each reader checking his or her own philosophy to see if what we are speaking agrees with his or her philosophy or another's philosophy. This is neither right, wrong, good, or bad. It creates a searching within each one of you. But a philosophy remains only a philosophy until it is lived, then it becomes a reality.

Every one of you, as a soul-god being, chose to be in a physical form for a reason, to learn to take your own divine spiritual essence and manifest it into physical matter, which is your creation. That is why we called you an aspect of God. God is an ancient word which simply means creative essence. And you are all creating. You are all taking what is called spirit, your spirit, the universal spirit within your soul essence, a soul consciousness, and you have chosen to place that energy within a human form in order to create with it.

But when that spirit is denied, the mind still creates. The mind is a collective consciousness of thoughts. When the mind creates without the heart, the end result of that creation is what you see outside called society.

When uniting with the heart, utilizing the mind and the heart in togetherness, the end result is freedom. The key is found in the humor of life and the laughter of life. The key to uniting the mind and heart is the utilization of the positive emotions. There needs to come a balance in this world, a balance of knowledge and wisdom, a balance of the knowledge of the mind, the intellect, with the wisdom of the heart. Indeed, you live in a world which has forgotten what balance is and what wisdom is. We are not saying this to you directly. We find that many of you are desiring inner wisdom and understanding.

What we are referring to is the mass consciousness in your world which has created such an imbalance of energy and nature. Those of you who are familiar with the laws of nature know that when there is an imbalance in nature, death occurs, death and rebirth, whether it is of the plant kingdom or the animal kingdom. And those of you who have studied scientifically within this realm understand this concept. When there is an imbalance between knowledge and wisdom, societies begin to die.

Your world has been presented with the option either of taking the wisdom of the heart essence and moving to the point of where intellectual knowledge is to create a balance, or of taking where knowledge is at this time and reverting back to the point of where wisdom is at this time. If the latter occurs, this will bring forth the fulfillment of many prophecies which have been given by many masters throughout your ages. Death, rebirth, and rejuvenation—you make a choice on what to experience.

One individual does not have to experience what the majority chooses. It is not correct to think that because everyone else is creating and choosing a particular event in your area, you must be involved in that event. That would remove free-will choice. One truly never loses one's free-will choice unless one gives one's power away to something or someone that says they want it. And many want it in this world. Many organizations teach fear. They teach that you need their organization or you will become lost. No, you won't! No soul is ever lost. The Universe knows where every soul is at all times. And assistance is given to every soul when it is requested.

There is no limit to the power of the mind or the power of your mind.

Perceive it in this manner: every one of you is an actress or an actor, you are a playwright, you are a producer and a director of a play, and your stage is the world. If you forget you are acting, you become lost in your own play. Remember who you are as a god, and that you are the creator of that play. You then do not become lost in the seriousness of what you are creating and experiencing. Some of you have even had souls written into the play, a friend to play the part of a villain. And the friend plays the role so well, you forget and you become angry at the villain.

Often what you would call your greatest enemy is also your greatest teacher, when you truly look at what you have attracted to you and why. Truly, there is nothing out there that can control you, alter you, or change you. With our words we will not have changed one mind because only you can change your mind. No one can truly ever change your mind. One can offer guidance, teaching, and assistance to you to change your mind, only if you desire to change your mind. But this is not from the perspective that you need to change your mind because you are wrong. This is very important to understand.

We desire no one to change because they are wrong. We see no one as wrong. Change because you desire to change, because you desire to begin experiencing new creations, new realities, and new experiences, and because you desire to begin coming to the point of experiencing the light of true joy and universal tranquility. Never has it been written in truth that a soul needs to experience pain in order to grow. Pain is a teacher, a rapid teacher sometimes, but so is true joy! True joy is also a teacher. And it is always your choice what to experience. The majority choose both pain and joy.

It is not wrong. It is your choice. As we said earlier regarding this play, you choose the subject matter of your own play. Some choose to experience a comedy, some a drama. But also understand, at any given moment in time you have the power to change your own play, to change your own characters which you have written in that play. You can do this by changing the thoughts you use to manifest that play. No one is a victim of society, but everyone has been programmed by your societies.

It is your choice how you experience, accept or deny that programming. Looking back to the issues of your own childhood, ask yourself, how much of your childhood can you remember? Then ask yourself, how much of your childhood do you want to remember?

Whenever there has been negative programming in the mind, whether it be called fear of loving, fear of survival, fear of guilt, fear of loss, fear of loneliness, or whatever the energy is of fear, we offer to you a tool in healing and removing that fear. This is done by entering into a meditative state, which is simply quieting the mind. For those of you who are more active in your physical movements, trying to sit still and meditate is often contradictory. You would benefit by walking in nature to meditate, or even by sitting near running water which creates movement next to you. This will assist you in meditation. And there are those of you who may simply desire to sit or to lie down and meditate in your own privacy.

As you enter into a meditative state, ask yourself to go back into your childhood to the point of origin of a fear. Some of you will see it. Some will feel it. Some will hear it while you are meditating and quieting the mind. The point is not just to see the effects of that particular fear, but to go to the point of origin. It could have been one week ago, or ten thousand lifetimes ago. The remembrance of that point of origin is still with you. Therefore, time is not an issue as to when it was created. As you go to the point of origin of that particular fear, seeing the event of the statement or the experience which programmed that fear into your mind, visualize a blanket of gold light going over the event. For some of you it would be easier to visualize sprinkling gold powder or gold sparkles over the event. While you are in the meditative state and doing this, you will feel the body becoming lighter. You will feel as if your own heart is beginning to grow, expand, and glow in light.

When you go back to the point of origin, the effects from that point of origin are placed in a process of healing. You will then begin finding yourself responding differently to events, to people, and to situations in your own life. And you will find a clarity coming to you regarding what you are choosing and why you are choosing it. Try it. It works.

If you want to find out why certain goals of yours are not being manifested, write down all of your fears, beginning with what you perceive as your greatest fear and ending with your lesser fears. Put the paper away for two to three days. Then, on another sheet of paper, write down your goals, beginning with your greatest goal and ending with what you would perceive as your lesser goals in life.

Compare the two columns. You will find that each goal corresponds with the same fear which is creating the blockage of that goal. You may not always be conscious that it was that particular fear.

You will find that after going back to the point of origin and releasing that fear during meditation, within four to twelve weeks after meditation that goal will begin the process of coming into physical manifestation.

But if you do this meditation exercise with the belief it will not work, then it will not work. Until you go back to the point when you first held that belief and heal the belief, it will not work. Indeed, one can have a bucket of water and cut a hole in the bottom and still stand all day trying to fill it up. That is the same concept as stating you want to achieve a goal but you also have the belief, "Well, it will never work anyway." Well, it won't. You are creating the belief that it will not work anyway. Therefore, that is one of your creations. It goes back to what we were speaking of earlier: what are you worth?

What are you worth receiving in this life? Recognize how many in the world have stated, "Well, God does not want me to have it anyway."

That is the same as one hand slapping your other hand. For, you are your own god. And your god, what's called your inner god, is not out there somewhere pulling strings, telling you what you have to do and what you don't have to do. Indeed, you are connected to your own higher-self, that part of you which is connected to the universal God essence. Even your physical conscious mind has free-will choice. Your soul has free-will choice, and your heart has free-will choice. You chose what to incarnate into. You chose what gender, what culture, what parents, what brothers or sisters, etcetera, to work with, to learn from, and to grow with.

And this gets back to what we were stating earlier, particularly for some of you who have such great difficulties with your parents, your children, your brothers, your sisters, or your mates. You wrote them into your own play. Begin going beyond that wall of seriousness and begin seeing the humor of life. Indeed, life is humorous when you see it from the overall perspective. When you see it from simply one point of view it can be greatly serious and painful. It is important to learn to bring in the vision of the totality of life by allowing the mind to expand.

There is another exercise you can utilize to begin to expand the mind, even the psychic ability of the mind. We utilize this word "psychic," which is a Greek word that simply means soul. Everyone is psychic. Not everyone gives oneself that power or credit, particularly with the focus your society has placed on what is called psychic. The mind is taught to attack what it fears, to attack it either physically, verbally, or mentally. That is why so many stay in what you call the closet.

You will study your beliefs and your spirituality as long as no one else knows it because the spirituality of freedom does create fear. If you tell a person who believes they are controlled by a judgmental god out there somewhere that they are free and that there is not a god out there who will punish them, it will then create fear and anger. They will attack because the mind has been programmed to believe what someone else says. They believe that someone else is more powerful than they are, when in truth all of you are in totality equal, just as we are equal with you.

There is no one greater than another. Indeed, this concept is contrary to the teachings of societies where one is greater, one is better, one is more spiritual, or whatever.

Now, back to the exercise. Get a paper, a cardboard shield, which is several feet in diameter. Have it be white in color with cardboard on the other side. Have the white colored side be the side close to you. Have different samples of colored paper. Hold one colored sample in your hand, one color at a time, with the other colors somewhere else. While you are sitting on the other side of this divider, close the eyes to visualize a beam of light coming forth from your third eye, that of the brow chakra, some call it the ajna. Have that beam of light that you are visualizing go through this white divider, touching the colored paper, and come back to you to give you the response. The more you practice this, the more you will begin finding that you know the color without seeing it with the physical eye. Indeed, this is but a simple exercise. It brings a little humor into what is called spirituality.

What you are doing is strengthening the ajna, the third eye. When this third eye is strengthened you can begin projecting into your environment and seeing what you are in the midst of creating in that environment, consciously and subconsciously. And you will come to find that there will no longer be surprises.

You have a term called accidents. We do not believe in accidents. But there are many surprises in life when one is not truly watching or looking at where one is going.

The power of the mind is unique in this particular school called Earth. This school is a school which teaches responsibility for all you do, all you think, and all you create. This is why so many have come to this school who are not responsible. They have come to learn what responsibility is.

The power of the mind is a wonderful tool with which to create a reality of joy. We hear the thoughts in certain minds as we speak this, "It may be true for another, but it is too hard for me to live a life of joy. That is a pipe dream."

What you can dream you can create, when you truly decide what you want. Indecision will create a reality of indecision. Be indecisive and what you attract to you is an indecisive energy called confusion. But also understand that in order to release and heal the trauma, pain, judgment, disease, or whatever it is you truly desire to heal, it cannot be healed when you are in the midst of judging it. Recognize that whatever event you wish to be healed, whatever relationship you desire to be healed, whatever condition of the body you desire to be healed, cannot be healed if you sit and judge that condition. It can only be healed when you come to love whatever it is that you desire to be healed.

For example, there are those who carry a disease and who desire that disease to be healed, yet they are constantly judging themselves or the disease. They cannot be healed until that disease becomes loved and the teaching that the disease is offering you is understood.

When we speak of judgment, we are referring to condemnation. We are not speaking of discernment in terms of judgment. Everyone needs to be able to discern what will be positive or negative for them based on their choices, to discern that going here or there or experiencing this or that should or should not be part of their reality. That is not judging. That is discernment.

When we utilize the word "judgment," we are speaking of condemning in a negative manner whatever it is one is judging. Therefore, if one is condemning that disease, they are not learning from it. They are not learning what created the disease. Therefore, the disease will not be healed.

Even physical death does not heal a disease. Death removes the physical tissue, yes, because the physical body has been removed. But the energy which created that disease is not healed simply because the body dies. Indeed, there is a concept in many spiritual movements that when one dies one is instantly enlightened. Why? The thoughts are there, the emotions are there, the memories are there. What has changed to make that particular soul instantly enlightened because one took off one's clothes called a body?

Now is the time to work on bringing forth your own enlightenment. Do you know that many infants who are born with diseases do so because they chose to reincarnate before they healed the disease? Most of the time it is still there. But that is not an absolute. There are some souls who will choose particular difficulties in order to teach the parents, to assist in awakening the spirit, the light within the parents. Many of the souls that your society label having Down Syndrome have come to teach the acceptance of loving which is not based on form, but based on spirit. Those persons who are repelled by someone with Down Syndrome are ones who fear within their own selves what is called loving. But this needs to be searched and discovered within each one individually.

Physical death does not create a healing simply because it was a physical death. There are many souls who have gone through the experience of physical death and they do not even know they have physically died. Many of these are in what is called the astral plane. These are commonly called ghosts who still live in houses because they think they still live there. They are living in their reality. They have not yet ascended to the Light. But again, this does not make a soul lost. Every soul is always assisted.

But also understand that if an individual dies of a disease it does not mean that this individual's soul does not ascend. Neither does it mean that the individual soul instantly goes into the astral plane and becomes a ghost! At any time, that soul can come to an understanding in the non-physical of the energy which created that disease, can come to accept the assistance available for healing that disease, and can ascend to the Light and have completed its cycles of development on the Earth plane. Again, there is no absolute. Every soul is different. Every circumstance is different. Every experience is different. What we are simply offering you is a general understanding by which you can begin searching from where you are.

Every one of you is different. Every one of you is special. Every one of you is loved unconditionally by the Universe, by the creative God essence. You do not have to do something, be something, or be somewhere to be loved unconditionally. You already are. But when that loving is denied down to the physical matter plane, that is the last stage of development in manifestation. When you see an event coming into physical form, you know that the event has been worked on for some time.

When it comes into physical form it is the last stage of manifestation of that particular event. Then comes the time when one questions, "Now, what will I do with it?" You need to ask what you have been doing with it.

Affirmations in accordance with the power of the mind are wonderful and sometimes work. Those of you who have tried affirmations time after time and do not find results, need to ask whether on the one hand your conscious mind is saying, "I deserve this to occur, and I ask it to occur out of love," while on the other hand, and at the same time, may be stating in your subconscious mind, "I deserve punishment. Do not allow this to occur."

When there is a conflict between the conscious and the subconscious, much stress begins building in the mind. When one denies one's emotions, stress begins building in the body. And if both of these are continued in suppression and denial, eventually one will experience a nervous breakdown, disease, depression, or other dysfunction.

Go to the subconscious of the mind. Do this through meditation, particularly when you have been affirming a particular event to transpire and it is not occurring. In deep meditation, visualize through your asking, "What is the belief of this affirmation by the subconscious of the mind?" And listen to what you hear.

If you hear opposition, ask at what time you began believing in that opposition, in that particular belief. Many times it will be in this life, in your own childhood. If it was in this life, in your own childhood, then visualize yourself as a child at that age when that was spoken to you. Then verbally, and it is important to do this verbally, begin speaking to this image of the child. You either see the image, hear the image, or feel the image. Begin asking this child if he or she fears you as an adult. Ask if this is a means by which this child is trying to punish the adult because he or she felt so punished by an adult? Begin teaching this child to love and accept him or herself unconditionally. Begin teaching this child, saying to this child, "You do not deserve punishment. You never need to prove yourself to anyone at any time."

Ask this child to become your friend. When a child has been traumatized, and the physical body of that child has become an adult, there is often a separation, where the child does not trust the adult, although both are within one body. They are different parts of the body and different parts of the mind. Thus, there will be energies trying to block what the adult conscious mind is trying to achieve. Some would call it self-sabotage. How that child felt towards adults is how that part of you, your personality feels toward you. There needs to come an attunement to yourself, the total self, to allow that healing to transpire. As you have reached this point of difficulty and you begin healing and coming into a harmonious relationship with your own inner child, you begin creating what you have been desiring to create and to achieve.

Every one of you is more than simply a conscious mind. Every one of you has more than one personality. Your personalities intermix and play off of each other, and sometimes are in competition with each other. This is also part of what we were speaking of earlier, of one part of you battling the other part or creating a reality of confusion. You need to learn to unite the totality of the self. And to unite the totality of the self, there needs to be the loving of who and what you are, without judging what you are or what you have created. Judge it, and it will not go away. It will become intensified.

This is so important to understand because what you project into your reality is what you will experience. Whatever you judge out there is going to come back unto you. The law of cause and effect and the power of the mind work both ways. The power of the mind can create heaven and it can create hell. Heaven and hell are states of mind. They are not geographical locations.

Many live in hell constantly. Indeed, what you see, feel, and think of yourself is what you will attract to yourself. That is why we continue to teach that there are no victims. Each one has made a choice, whether that choice be of the conscious mind, the subconscious mind, or even the soul mind. But also, it is important to understand that even though there are no victims, that does not mean there is not to be loving and compassion for those who are in pain. That does not mean you do not go and assist ones who are in pain. So often we have read in the minds, "They are not a victim. They created it. They can fix it."

Allow the human heart's compassion to return to your societies, to allow the loving of one another to return to your societies. It begins within yourself, with what you are.

Some of you will experience changes for the positive, beginning immediately. Some, in weeks to come. Some, in years to come. And some, in lifetimes to come. We have spoken here to more than just your conscious mind. We have spoken to your subconscious mind and to your own soul mind. Some of you do not consciously understand all we have said. That is neither right, wrong, good, nor bad.

There is never a judgment of right or wrong regarding what each one of you choose to experience. Indeed, this is your life, your play, and you, and only you, have the power to change it from a drama to a comedy, to begin truly seeing the humor of life. Yes, there are major difficulties in your world. There are millions in your world who are dying by the hour. There are also millions being born by the hour.

Death and rebirth, change, teaching, and learning … never think that you cannot assist in changing the world. But know that before you can assist in creating change upon the Earth, the change must first occur within you. We are not speaking of you changing the mind or the philosophy of the world. When you begin changing yourself, that is when you begin assisting in changing the mass consciousness of your world.

Each one of you carries a light within you. There will come a time for some of you when that light ignites and glows with brilliance. It already has in some of you. Again, that does not make one better or worse. Every time one ignites one's own inner light, two more begin searching. You are all students because you are all teachers.

Indeed, as we have said before, a philosophy is only a philosophy until it is lived, then it becomes a reality. The dream which one had can become a reality when one believes one is worth it. And it is important to ask what you are worth. The answer to that question is that you are worth the Universe because the Universe is your heritage. You are simply here on a temporary basis, in a temporary body, learning, growing, and creating. Some had a traumatic birth and developed spiritual amnesia. Many are beginning to come out of that spiritual amnesia and are beginning to remember their heritage, to remember their true family. Those of you who have had an aching inside of you, truly wanting to know where your family is, a family you truly feel connected to, and wanting to know where your home is because you have never truly felt at home, this understanding comes to you upon your own awakening from spiritual amnesia.

We are giving you exercises which are not absolutes. They are simply tools. The exercises in and of themselves will do nothing but create curiosity. What is important is the belief, not in us nor in something out there, but the belief in yourself, the belief that you have the power to change what you desire to change. Every one of you who is reading this has this ability. It is up to you what you will do with it. The choice is always yours.

There is no one out there who can ever do it for you. But there are many gods who will assist you for eternity, if need be. But never is there one who will do it for you. That is your job, your responsibility. Whatever you perceive needs to be fixed, realize that you are the one who broke it.

Utilize the power of the mind to create a reality of joy. Are you worth it? Indeed, all of you are worth it. You never have to do anything to be worth life. You simply are life. Indeed, all of you need to make choices. And you do this constantly. You do it over a thousand times a day. Most of the time you are not even aware that you have made a choice, but you do it constantly.

Come to know the choices you are making which result in the reality you are experiencing. These exercises will assist you in understanding these choices and why you made them, and in coming to love all that you are and all you have created.

There is no void in energy. If a negative creation is not filled with an energy of love and of light, it will be filled again with an energy of negativity or of lesser light. Whenever you are removing an obstacle you cannot leave a void. Everything you seek to release, do so by loving it, and that love will begin neutralizing the negative energy. Judge it, and you will increase the negativity and make it stronger. Whatever you judge out there, you make stronger in here, you make stronger the negative energy which is in you.

For the next two days allow your conscious mind to pay close attention to whatever is attracted to your environment and to your space, whether it be a new person, an old person, a new attitude in an old person, whether it be someone in your automobiles stopping in front of you, whether it be a leaf falling or the wind blowing across the face and hair. For the next two days, ask the mind to be aware of all that occurs in your environment, in your space. And every event which transpires in that time which you did not like, record it, particularly the events which are perceived as more major than others. Search out why you did not like that event inside of yourself. State it in this manner. The event which occurred in your space and in your environment you did not like is telling you that the event is a mirror, a reflection of something in you which you do not like. And it is a tool of showing you, of teaching you to search within that nature of you, and of what you do not like.

On the other end of the scale, all the events which occurred in your space during that period of time that you truly liked are telling you things in you that you like. The purpose in doing this is to bring a greater expanded awareness of what you create every day of your life in your environment. There is not one event, regardless of how minute, which is brought into your environment which you have not created. Even stubbing the toe is an event you created, perhaps with a very minute subconscious reason for it. But whenever you begin having many minor accidents, for example, this is telling you something. This is telling you that you are beginning to create a major accident. You might call it a surprise.

By taking these two days to begin focusing on all the events you have attracted to your environment, you will become more in tune with what you are attracting to you, what level of energy you are attracting to you. By seeing your environment, you are seeing the mirror of yourself. Indeed, we have often made the statement that there are truly only seven souls upon the Earth, and the rest is done with mirrors! The symbology of this statement means there are seven levels, seven types of consciousness, or even call it seven levels, seven types of personalities, each one in their own schooling experience, schooling meaning your experience of incarnations upon the Earth. The Earth school is one in which you will experience all levels of these personalities, you will experience all levels of these consciousnesses, not necessarily in one lifetime, although some do. In this way, you are constantly meeting yourself. This is indeed a philosophy on which to ponder. How many times do you meet yourself each day?

7

The Power of Meditation

The power of meditation is a tool and technique to assist you in reaching the core of the inner realm in which your chosen destiny lies. It can assist you in moving aside the intellect, that part of the mind which attempts through belief systems to separate out one's power and one's destiny.

In ancient times, the power of meditation was also referred to as prayer, prayer to the inner god and the inner part of your being which connects you with the God-force of the Universe, the creative force. Destiny was also an ancient term related to the creative force, the God-force, and the Universal Mind. Your chosen destiny was how you chose to manifest, how you chose to experience and explore multiple realms, inner dimensions, and realities of life.

There is as an ancient scripture in your book called the Bible which says to pray continuously. It says to constantly be in prayer. The meaning of constantly being in a state of prayer, a state of awareness, or a state of meditation, does not mean to simply sit in the chair your entire life or to stay in bed your entire life. Indeed, it does not. The state of meditation is a state of mind and a state of heart. It is being in a state of awareness in which you know who, what, and why you are. It is claiming your power and your identity.

Being in a constant state of meditation is being constantly aware of your environment, it is being constantly aware of the subtle energies and the subtle messages. It is not too difficult for the conscious mind to be aware of dramatic messages and dramatic energies. But the dramatic is not always there. The majority of the time, subtle energies and messages are in and around you continuously. But when one does not pay attention to the subtle energies and messages, many of these build into a major message or major experience. And sometimes this experience can be quite painful.

When one listens to the subtle messages, one becomes aware of the creative process within their beingness. One becomes aware of one's own inner chosen destiny and how it is being fulfilled, how it is manifesting.

The power of meditation is the power which unites the mind and the heart. Later on in this chapter we will offer a guided meditation. But this is not all there is to meditation. The guided meditation is given simply to assist you in allowing the mind to relax and the heart to be expressed. It is given to assist in uniting both the mind and heart through the expression of unconditional loving.

The guided meditation is simply a tool to assist you in beginning to feel what it is like to be in a deep state of meditation, and then to take that feeling and allow it to be expressed through your beingness throughout the day, even throughout your night. Because you, as a being, are continuously expressing. Whether you are awake or asleep, you are still expressing your beingness. The power of meditation is a tool which allows you to truly feel.

As you breathe during the meditation, allow yourself to feel the power of breath, the power of life, and the power of creation. How many of you walk around each day habitually breathing yet do not consciously recognize you are breathing, unless you overexert yourself and become out of breath? It is then that the consciousness pays quite a bit of attention to one's breathing, to the breath. Allow yourself to feel the breath which enters into your beingness and through your beingness; allow yourself to feel the expansion of the lungs; allow yourself to feel the movement of blood in your body; allow yourself to feel life.

Many in your society allow themselves to be controlled by emotional reactions. Many will state, "I do express my emotions. Every time I get angry I express my emotions."

That is not the same as feeling. Emotional reactions are reactions to a belief system. That is being in a mode of survival. And you as humans, as the human consciousness, are truly here to learn to move beyond the mode of survival into a mode of knowingness and living.

In a culture that is so caught up in the rise of intellectualism, in analyzing life, taking life and separating it, placing it within categories and boxes, so many deny feelings. Your true feelings are the expression of the inner self coming forth, the feeling of being involved, involved with the power of creation. Your true feelings are those feelings of power within you, the feelings that allow lovingness to manifest, the feelings that allow compassion to manifest, the feelings that allow the Christed-consciousness to be expressed through you as a human being, the feelings of joy and laughter. And these feelings are in every soul.

In this culture, the majority of what one creates is created on an unconscious level because so many deny their feelings. And expressing one's feelings is not going to someone you do not like and simply telling them off, and then perceive, "I have expressed my feelings." That is not expressing your feelings. That is demonstrating your own judgment and fear of your own self. The expression of feelings that we are speaking of is the expression of the Christ energy, the Christed-consciousness. That has nothing to do with religion. It has everything to do with spirituality.

Place reminders to yourself in your environment. Write notes to yourself. Place them around your home. Place on the note, "How does it feel to breathe? How did that last breath feel?" When one allows oneself to feel one's physical essence, then one truly begins feeling one's spiritual essence. But so often what we find is commercialized spiritualism, where many go about constantly trying to feel spirituality, to project spirituality out there, to have an out-of-body experience, to have a vision of something out there, running to and fro hunting for the extraterrestrials! Yet they are not allowing themselves their own beingness, to feel their own physicalness, or to be grounded and centered in the moment.

How can one feel one's spiritual essence if one is not feeling one's physical essence, the physical essence which is the tool for spiritual expression in this plane of existence?

The power of meditation is tuning into that power source by the means of the breath of life, the power of life, and by allowing yourself to feel all parts of your body. How many in your society walk around with diseases which they are not even aware that they carry? They go to doctors who take many tests, and the doctors come back and tell them they have a disease. This lack of awareness is because they are not allowing themselves to feel.

As you feel your body, your essence, as you allow yourself to feel every cell of the body, you then know exactly what is transpiring in your body. You know exactly where any tensions are being held in the body. You know exactly where you are allowing that breath to enter into the body, or even where you are not allowing it to enter into the body.

When ones enter into emotional reactions, meaning, when ones enter into a state of survival mode, the body begins holding on to negative tensions. This can occur in any part of the body, or numerous parts of the body. Where that energy of tension is held and constricted in the body, it is denying breath to enter into that part of the body. The tension blocks the life-force energy in that part of the body. And eventually, if this is done long enough, that part of the body will become diseased because it is not at-ease with the flow of the life-force energy. Rather, it is at dis-ease with the life-force energies.

The guided meditation we offer in this chapter is simply a tool, a guide for you to enter into that state and allow yourself to feel. The purpose of this particular guided meditation is to assist you in releasing the negative contracted energy called tension which is held in certain parts of the body.

The meditation is to assist you in recognizing what parts of the body are holding on to the tension. In releasing the tension from those parts of the body, you will begin feeling in those parts of the body.

Whatever part of the body has been denied feelings relates to the part of your creative force which you are also denying. You are also denying that part of your creative power. You are denying living.

And then one moves further into the mode of survival. When ones are in the mode of survival, you find the minds becoming contracted. That is when you find minds becoming controlling and filled with anger, fear, and eventually disease because they are not at-ease with the flowing essence of the life-force energy.

The power of meditation is a tool to move you into a state of feeling. As we stated earlier, when you are in that state of feeling, the power of your creation, your creative essence, your creative energy, magnifies and multiplies. You begin feeling a joy in living. You begin feeling the purpose in life, your purpose in life, your personal purpose in life which you and you alone choose.

In this guided meditation, focus on your breathing. Take a breath and allow that breath to go deeply into the body until you feel that breath of life go to the toes of the feet. Begin allowing yourself to feel the entire body breathe. Allow yourself to feel, taking in breath through the organ called the skin. Allow yourself to feel the totality of your body breathe and become at one with that breath. The power of meditation is the key to entering into that state of altering your reality, of entering into the inner realms in which lies the core of your inner destiny. When you become at one with the knowingness of that inner destiny, then the doors will open wide and clear for you to walk through. The fog will no longer be, it will have dissipated. And the veil of the illusion will no longer be because the core of your beingness and the core of your chosen destiny begin coming into physical manifestation.

In this meditation, remember to breathe. Even as you are reading or listening to the words in this guided meditation, allow yourself to feel the movement of that breath in every cell of the body. And enjoy your journey to your inner destiny.

Guided Meditation

Place your body in a comfortable position. It does not matter whether it is in a sitting position or a lying position. Allow yourself to feel the tensions departing from the top of the head, from the scalp. Allow your eyes to relax and become unfocused. Allow the ears and the jaw to relax. Allow the neck and the shoulders to relax. Allow your arms, your hands and your fingers to relax. Allow your spine to relax, especially your lower spine. Allow your hips to relax. Now, allow your legs to relax and your feet to relax, and your toes to relax.

Take a deep breath into the body, and then exhale the same length of time it took you to take in the breath. Breathe the next breath even deeper. Exhale longer. With each breath you take, allow the body to become more relaxed.

Allow your mind to scan your body. Search which part of the body is not relaxing at this point. As you breathe in even deeper, allow your mind to search your body from head to toe. Ask yourself which part of the body is not relaxing.

Take another breath, breathing even deeper, exhaling longer. Continue the deep breathing until the breath goes to the toes and the feet. Still, be mindful of where the tension is being held in the body. Be mindful of which part of the body is not relaxing. Continue breathing deeper and deeper and deeper. Allow yourself to feel the expansion of the lungs. Allow yourself to begin feeling your heart beating.

Now, take a breath, and breathe that breath to the part of the body where tension is held. Visualize the breath surrounding the tension in the body. As you exhale, breathe out that tension. Exhale the tension out of the body. Continue doing this by working one part of the body at a time. Begin with the area of the body which carries the greatest tension, and continue working on that part of the body, breathing in, surrounding the tension, and exhaling the tension out of the body. Continue each breath, one after another, to that part of the body until the tension is no longer in that part of the body.

If you are finding tension in another part of the body, breathe to that part of the body and exhale the tension from that part of the body. At the same time, allow yourself to feel the movement of that breath as it enters into the body, as it expands the lungs.

Allow yourself to feel the beating of the heart.

Again, take a deep breath. Now, begin visualizing your entire body breathing. Begin visualizing all the surface area of your skin breathing in that breath of life. Visualize the breath of life being breathed in through the skin, and visualize the oxygen you are breathing in beginning to turn into a golden light.

As you breathe in through the skin, exhale through the mouth. As you visualize your skin breathing in the golden light, allow your body to feel lighter and lighter and lighter. Visualize that gold light collecting all of the negative thoughts, the pain, the suffering, and the tensions. As you exhale through your mouth you are releasing those old thoughts, you are releasing that pain, suffering, and tension.

Each time you breathe in through the skin and exhale through the mouth, the body is becoming lighter and lighter and lighter. Continue to allow yourself to feel the beating of your heart. If you do not feel the beating of the heart, visualize the golden light to increase, and create an even greater lightness of the body.

The lighter the body becomes, the easier one can feel the beating of the heart. Allow your mind to focus on that golden light and still allow yourself to feel the beating of the heart.

Breathe deeper and deeper and deeper. As you are breathing in that golden light, visualize that it is creating a light so that you may see the core of your inner being. Visualize the core of your inner being as a golden ray of light which is in the center of your beingness, in the center of your body. If you are not yet quite seeing that core or ray of light, continue breathing in that golden light through the skin. And as you continue breathing, it will bring more light into the body. You will begin seeing the inner core of your inner beingness.

Continue to allow yourself to feel the beating of the heart. Visualize the ray of golden light pulsating within your center. Visualize the ray pulsating with the beating of the heart, and allow the two to become as one. Visualize that ray of golden light pulsating greater and greater and greater. Visualize yourself becoming one with the golden ray of light within you, beating as one with the heart.

As you feel the pulsating light, allow yourself to begin communicating with that pulsating golden light within you, that core of your inner being. Allow yourself to go into that ray of pulsating golden light. Allow yourself to feel the beating of the heart. Allow yourself to communicate with the core of light within you. Allow yourself to become one with the golden light within you.

The more you allow the light to pulsate in harmony with the beating of the heart, the more you are able to communicate with this part of your beingness. Allow yourself to feel the answers to your questions come from this pulsating light within you. Allow yourself to feel your inner truth. Allow yourself to feel your inner knowingness. Allow yourself to feel oneness with the Universe and the God essence.

Ask at this time to be released from separation and to see yourself as that core ray of light pulsating with the beating of the heart, becoming one with the Universe. Allow yourself to feel your inner truth, your inner knowing, and the empowerment of your inner being.

Inhale even deeper and deeper and deeper. Allow yourself to continue communicating with that ray of light. Listen to the answers with your feelings. Know that those inner feelings will lead you well. Allow yourself to feel that truth. Allow yourself to feel the oneness of the God essence, the oneness of the universal mind. Allow yourself to feel the power of loving yourself because you are one with all there is. You are one with the light, the harmony, the beauty, and the peace of the Universe.

As you continue breathing, continue to allow yourself to feel the beating of the heart. Continue communicating with that light because that light is you. That light is the core of your destiny. That light is what bonds you to the Universe. Being within that light is what brings you into your knowingness, your wisdom, and your equality within the God essence of life.

Continue lying there, or sitting there, and continue communicating with that light. Continue asking questions about your destiny, about your oneness, and about your role in the family called the Universe.

Continue your breathing and communicating until you feel naturally inclined to come out of this state.

Remember this state. Remember feeling this state throughout your life in whatever you do.

Continue this breathing meditation until you allow yourself to feel the beating of the heart with the pulsating of the core light, the golden light. When you feel the beating of the heart with the pulsating of the light, this is a sign that you have opened the door and you have removed the veil to your inner knowingness. Continue working toward this.

Each time you do this meditation it will become deeper and deeper and deeper. And the deeper you go, the more you bring forward to your conscious state, and the more you can be in a continuous state of meditation and harmony.

8

Sexuality

Sexuality, such a topic of discussion! Not only will we cover the physical aspect of sexuality, but also the attitudes carried in your world consciousness and social consciousness about sexuality. We will also discuss sexuality with regards to the subconscious mind.

Sexuality is an activity and an energy, an exchange of energy. It is an energy which can bring an intensity of joy and union when understood. Yet there is such fear. The mind holds fear of the great taboos that society has placed upon sexuality. The subconscious mindset of your social attitudes still lives in the Victorian Age, although these attitudes did not begin in the Victorian Age. Indeed, they began in the age of Atlantis.

Sexuality is simply an exchange of energy. It is an exchange of energy in accordance to yin and yang, and in accordance to male and female energies. We are not referring to your physical forms called man and woman, we are referring to male energy and female energy. Male energy is a creative energy. Female energy is an energy of receptivity.

It is important to understand that every physical man carries male and female aspects, and every physical woman carries male and female aspects. Therefore, do not allow confusion in the consciousness about male or female energy, or think that one is greater than another. Neither one is greater than the other. There is not one male in physical form greater than any female in physical form. Your society is beginning to recognize this, although it is still dragging its feet.

Indeed, you are coming to understand that all that exists is equal. Yes, there are ones with more knowledge and more wisdom, but that does not make one greater. All that exists, physical and non-physical, is equal.

However, not all that exists in the physical is in balance. And when there is an imbalance of energy created between the male and female aspects within a particular individual, there are difficulties created in the expression and enjoyment of sexuality. When sexuality is utilized as a control, as a way of forcing oneself upon another, it is demonstrating a lack of balance between the male and female energies.

Sexuality is not wrong, nor is sexuality a sin. An understanding is needed in your plane of existence that sexuality is a part of the physical life and should not be denied out of fear or out of separation from your emotions, your God-self, or your creative self.

As we stated earlier, sexuality is an exchange of energy. When one individual is having a sexual relationship with another individual, they are creating an exchange of life-force energies, one unto each other. But also understand that when one is having a sexual relationship with another and the attitude of fear exists, the attitude of control exists, the attitude of separation exists, or the attitude of guilt exists, then that is the energy being exchanged.

That energy thus begins creating a blockage. If the blockage is not recognized or understood, then the blockage will result in a disease. Most of the time the disease chosen would be a sexual disease for both involved in the sexual relationship.

Hidden guilt, hidden fears, and hidden frustrations have been a part of your existence. Whether these exist in the conscious or the subconscious, whether the energies come from this incarnation or another incarnation, there must come the resolution of your own sexual identity. Your own sexual freedom of expression needs to come into being without control and manipulation. As we stated earlier, you need to understand the yin and the yang, which are opposite polarities, and you need to allow growth to occur.

True growth does not start on one particular end and journey to another end. True growth begins on both ends and comes equally to the center. Another way of stating this is that true growth is coming to the center of your own God-beingness, coming to know your own spiritual nature, and coming to know yourself. Indeed, the majority of you in this world do not even know your own self because of fears about coming to know who you are. You carry such fears of coming to understand why you have certain feelings and certain thoughts, particularly with regards to sexuality. Such an array of thoughts that transpire in your minds! Such fear and guilt are held with these thoughts that they are pushed away into the subconscious mind because you refuse to look at them. You refuse to see where they are coming from. You refuse to look at yourself.

Then you sit in judgment of yourself. Self-judgment blocks the growth of the yin and yang, the opposite polarities. The growth does not journey to the center. One begins growing on one end while the other end grows at a slower rate of speed. This creates an imbalance. The imbalance of energies then allows you to be susceptible to the energies of the mass consciousness, the world consciousness, and the social consciousness. These are all one and the same. The energies of fear and guilt begin creating imbalances in the psychological development, the human consciousness.

Many of you begin to allow your imagination to rule what you desire to create. Do not misunderstand here, however. There is nothing wrong with the imagination. Indeed, you cannot imagine anything you have not experienced to one degree or another. We are not stating that because you have imagined you have actually done that event. But when you have imagined an event, you have indeed experienced the energy of that event.

While many of you outwardly carry guilt about something, you utilize your imagination to escape in fantasies. The guilt then creates a blockage of your own sexual energies. When those energies are carried while you are having a sexual relationship with another person, you transmit that energy to the other.

The other is not a victim, however. The other is allowing it. As we have taught before, there are no victims. What you carry in your mind, whether it is positive or negative, you are working on the process of drawing it to yourself, no matter what the event is which you constantly carry in the mind. Therefore, if you do not desire a negative event to happen to you, then cease dwelling on the negative event! Cease dwelling on the fear!

What we are speaking of here is what you would term rape, for example, the forcing of a sexual encounter upon another without their conscious permission. This is allowing the darkness of the mind to overpower what you, as a god, are. Rape is an energy that has been suppressed for a long time. It is not so much for sexual gratification as it is for the need to demonstrate control over another. Indeed, that is why the majority of those who are raped are in female form because the male form in your society has been taught that they are superior.

Are they greater? Such ignorance in understanding what equality is! It is also important to understand the word "karma." What you create will return to you, if not in this incarnation, then in another. The only way to release karma is to learn the acceptance of the Christ-self, which is loving yourself unconditionally. When this is achieved, all karma is released.

Sexual energy within an individual is not limited to the sexual organs. Sexual energies are directly connected to the emotional body. The emotional body exists in all of you, not just in one part of the body. When there is a blockage, when there is difficulty in the expression of emotions, then this begins creating a blockage in sexuality. Therefore, the main focus in healing this is not just on sexuality, it is on your own emotional being-ness. You need to focus on the guilt you carry, whether it is regarding sexuality or another matter.

There needs to be a healing of the emotions, a discussion of the emotions, a discussion with yourself and by yourself. This requires being honest with yourself. Do you know how to do this? Do you know how to be honest with yourself? Be assured it is possible. The mind of mankind seeks to continue lying to itself and deceiving itself. The mind has such an ability to deceive its own self. The body always works in honesty. The body does not deceive. The body is a direct manifestation of your thoughts, your attitudes, and your reflections of yourself.

When ones are attracted to a body, they are attracted to what they see within themselves, whether they want to be or not. Couples in a marriage relationship act as mirror to each other. Like it or not, it is the truth. If you do not like it, then begin looking at that aspect you do not like and ask yourself why. In fact, the energy of the consciousness, the aspect of the personality you see in your mate that you do not like is simply showing you there is the same thing in you that you do not like. Whether it is conscious or subconscious, it still exists.

There is such judgment in your world regarding sexuality, of what is right, wrong, good, and bad. What you call homosexuality and bisexuality is not a sin, is not wrong, even though many judge these as wrong. And those of you who seek to sit in judgment of this statement, understand this, and understand this well, you judge homosexuality and bisexuality because you fear it may exist in you, consciously or subconsciously. Such fear that rules the mind! Such fear that rules judgment! Such ignorance that would judge loving!

There is not just one answer to the question of what creates homosexuality. Souls exist both in the male and female form. When one has existed many times in a female form, for example, and then chooses to experience the reality of a male form, there are still certain patterns, certain desires, to which it has become accustomed that would make the soul sexually desire a male form. Is it right? Wrong? Indeed not. It is neither. It is a learning experience. But also understand this—it is neither right or wrong between the male and female, a man and a woman. It is also a learning experience.

When sexuality occurs it is to be for a purpose of sharing lovingness, not simply for conscious gratification out of the energy of lust where the heart is not involved. The latter energy does and will create disease. If it doesn't create a physical sexual disease, it will indeed create a disease of the mind called guilt, fear, and anger.

There is nothing wrong with two men or two women living in a relationship where they love each other from the heart, are seeking to learn from each other from the heart, and are utilizing the expression of sexuality, an exchange of energy between each other. But so many of those termed homosexuals accept such fear and guilt from this society. So many desire to hide in the closets, fearing greatly they will be found out. So many have sexual experiences with ones they do not even know. The fear and guilt they carry is the basis of disease.

This also occurs between men and women. Fearing a commitment of a relationship, fearing the expression of the heart, many seek to run about in your streets, hiding in the dark rooms simply for the purpose of sexuality. This will also create disease. Indeed, what you are exchanging are your fears, your inhibitions, and your frustrations. Understand this well, my friends, it is not the act of sexuality itself, it is the purpose and the reason behind the act of sexuality that makes it positive or negative.

Sexuality assists in the movement of the Kundalini. Do you know of the Kundalini? It is the life-force energy that moves from the base chakra to the crown chakra. It connects all the chakras with the flow of life, the flow of energy, the acceptance of the universal energy force, and the enjoyment of life in totality. Sexuality, when exchanged from the heart, assists in moving the Kundalini. But also, on the opposite end, when sexuality is exchanged without the lovingness of the heart, it blocks the Kundalini. It blocks the flow of the life-force energies. And when the life-force energy is blocked, disease is created.

You do not need to experience disease. Is it not time to begin coming to know yourself and understand yourself? Is it not time to come to love yourself unconditionally and to utilize the tool of sexuality to assist you in this? Is it not time to learn to love sexuality and see it as part of the God-force, not just a means to recreate physical forms so that other souls can enter into the physical plane? Is it not time to learn the expression of the true God-self?

Does sexuality exist in the non-physical? Many have asked this question. The answer is yes, it does. But the sexual organs are not utilized. The energies blend as if creating a spark of life, which is like a sexual encounter, even in the non-physical.

Now, many wonder whether sexuality should be taught to children. Many wonder when this should be taught and by whom. Sexuality is a subject that should never be hidden from children. What we are referring to here is the teaching of what sexuality is, the teaching to respect sexuality, and the teaching to the consciousness not to fear or be inhibited by sexuality.

Understand that a newborn infant begins learning in the consciousness immediately. All discussions held around an infant enter into the human consciousness, although they will not be remembered consciously. Indeed, all is recorded in the subconscious. Whatever attitudes or fears are spoken of at that time will be a part of the subconscious of that infant. Nothing is ever forgotten at any time, ever.

When you begin teaching children about sexuality, teach them not to fear it, judge it, or condemn it. Instead, teach responsibility in accordance with sexuality. Teach the children not to allow others to force sexuality upon them. So many parents hold fears regarding sexuality, and they fear teaching it to their children

The consciousness of children, from time to time, listens to an adult, or even another child, who seeks to force sexuality upon a child. Why do you think there has been so much sexual abuse on children? This is not new. It is not new. Fear begets fear. When a child absorbs the fear of the parent regarding sexuality, then that child will draw to himself or herself an energy of fear from another regarding sexuality.

These experiences do not need to be experienced. When you take an infant and begin teaching that infant the respect of sexuality, the honor of sexuality, and the balance of sexuality, when you teach the child that there never needs to be guilt involved with sexuality, you will see that infant, the consciousness of that infant, come into a great balance of compassion, lovingness and understanding. And know that even you as adults who have carried fear, judgment, anger, and frustration regarding sexuality, can also heal your conscious and subconscious mind.

As in the meditations we spoke of before, return to the age when the fear began. This would be of assistance to you. You may find this age by entering into a meditation, by quieting the mind.

Visualize a sea of water as smooth as glass surrounding you. Then, ask the sea of glass at what age, during which incident did you begin fearing sexuality? That age will appear as a reflection in the water to tell you what age to begin meditating. When you have that particular age, visualize in the third eye yourself at that age. Begin speaking to this child as if it were a physical child sitting in front of you. Teach that child never to fear. Teach that child never to judge. Teach that child to love itself, all aspects of itself, including the loving of its own physical body.

In doing this you are creating a direct link between your conscious and your subconscious mind to heal and cleanse the negative energy in your subconscious mind. Understand that sexuality is to be enjoyed. Sexuality is not to be limited simply because of the limited beliefs you have accepted.

In the sexual act itself is the uniting of the energies of the soul that will never be forgotten in all eternity. It unites the energies of the soul and creates what is like a shield of great strength around yourself that cannot be impregnated by any outside force of negativity. Indeed, it is as if you are putting on armor so that no one can destroy you. The sexual act unites the heart chakras. With the sensations that exist in your physical form regarding sexual energies, is the opening of the heart chakra, the blending and uniting of the heart chakras, when the purpose of this sexual act is out of loving and sharing, not out of greed, lust, anger, revenge, control, or fear.

When sexual acts occur, and these energies of negativity exist, they begin closing the heart chakra. Do you understand what is yin and yang? Opposite polarities of growth must grow in equal measure, from both ends to the center. You need to grow to find your own centeredness, your own God-self, your own creative self.

What you call impotence is simply an energy that is blocked. It is blocked because of fear and guilt. The fear and guilt do not need to be associated with sexuality. It can be fear and guilt about any activity, any event. Fear and guilt both create a disturbance in the life-force energies. It is as if an energy comes into the bodies, the seven bodies that each of you have, and this energy of fear and guilt begins creating a shell around the emotional body. It creates a rigidity in the emotional body. It blocks the movement, the expansion of the emotional body. Physically, it would be as if you were wearing a straight jacket which would limit your movement, and which would create a sense of claustrophobia. Guilt and fear create claustrophobia in the emotional body, they inhibit the movement. When the emotional body is inhibited, a blockage of the flow of sexuality is created.

To heal the emotional body one needs to journey to the point of action and reaction that started this process of inhibiting the emotional body. Recreate the event into a positive event and you begin a process of healing the psychological aspect of the human conscious. One of the difficulties with your world psychologists and psychiatrists lies with their failure to understand the seven bodies. They do not understand how the seven bodies work together. They do not understand how they are intermixed and interblended. They do not understand that if one of the seven bodies is injured, it will affect the rest. On a physical level, it is as if your thumb was cut off from your hand and a doctor began working on your toes, trying to heal the difficulty!

All seven bodies must be recognized. We have spoken of these seven bodies before, in Chapter Three. And you must recognize that the seven bodies are not separated. When you exist in separation, the denial of the life energies exists and you begin dying. Whether you are dying emotionally, spiritually, mentally, or physically, you are still dying. Indeed, everyone needs the life-force energies of the Universe to sustain life.

It is important to understand the significance of the emotional body in direct correlation with sexuality. When you fear your emotions, you fear sexuality. One can fear the emotions consciously, but fear sexuality subconsciously, and vice versa. Know that assistance is available to all of you at all times, but you must be willing to ask for it. And after you have asked for it you must be willing to receive it, whether it is the healing of the physical body, the healing of the emotional body, the healing of yourself presently, or the healing of yourself as a child. Allow the heart to be blended with another.

Also, we will speak of celibacy. We well recognize that some in your world desire to teach that being a celibate makes you more spiritual. Such fear and ignorance that seek to separate the emotional body! It's like saying, "Just exist in the mental body without the heart." Never has it ever been taught in truth that one needs to be celibate to become spiritual. And be assured, Jeshua, the one the world calls Jesus, was not celibate. Indeed, those who truly understand spirituality will not be surprised by this statement. Jeshua was an avatar, a master, before he came into physical form. Therefore, why would he need to be celibate to become spiritual?

Sexuality does not decrease your spirituality when it comes from the heart. On the contrary, sexuality assists in increasing and enhancing your own spirituality when sexuality comes from the heart, from a uniting of the hearts, and is in total agreement with the heart. This is not to be used as an excuse, however, that because you desire to become more spiritual you need to force your mate to have more sex! It must be of a mutual agreement and mutual desire. Indeed, there must be openness of communication of all your feelings to each other. That is a part of life.

Understand this well—there are no secrets, only delayed information. And the delayed information is only for a short time. What you seek to hide from another, you are simply delaying until another comes to know it. There are no secrets, be assured.

Sexuality can and does heal the emotional body. As we stated earlier, when the sexual act is created in accordance with the heart, it not only unites the heart chakras as one heart chakra, it also moves, raises, the Kundalini. As the Kundalini rises, the veil drops. The veil that hides the universal awareness from your consciousness begins dissipating. The more the Kundalini rises, the less dense the veil is. Remember this.

Becoming a master is a continual process. A soul never stops learning at any time. For all eternity a soul will never stop growing or learning. There is no end. There is only life and the fulfillment of life, the fulfillment of laughter, and the joy of life. Is it not well past time that you drop your veil, your façade, your illusion, your inhibitions, your ignorance of life, and your judgment of life of who is right and who is wrong?

Indeed, there are many teachers without physical bodies who are coming to your Earth plane to teach. There are many teachers because there are many different levels of consciousness to be taught. Each teacher chooses and works with a particular level of consciousness.

We have chosen to come here and work with the consciousness, to teach the human consciousness that there is no limitation. My friends, we have not come here to your Earth plane to change your beliefs. Only you can change you. We have come to your Earth plane to teach you that pain is not of necessity, to teach you of your own godship, to assist you to return back to your own god source, and to teach that true joy indeed may be known. We are here to offer a light to you so you may see your pathway and that of your own light, so that spark within you might ignite into a great flame to guide and direct you, that you will become your own teacher and your own student.

All of you carry that spark of God in you. What you do with that spark is up to you—to allow that spark to become as a flame to lighten the pathway of your own knowingness, or to hide the spark away. That spark of God is eternal. Your consciousness is eternal. Your memories are eternal. Whether this is understood and believed at this time or after ten thousand lifetimes makes no difference. You are not here running a race. You are here to learn of your truth.

Your world teaches that one must first learn how to crawl, then one must learn how to walk, then one can learn how to fly. But we are here to teach you that by simply knowing that you can fly, you can fly. We are not here to give you thirty, fifty, or one hundred steps to enlightenment. If we gave you this, and you would take all of these steps, whether you do it in one lifetime or ten thousand lifetimes, you would still be reading the small print in books wondering if you did this or that step right.

Enlightenment can occur, and often does occur, in the twinkling of an eye, when you believe it can. You do not need to follow multiple steps to find enlightenment. You simply need to love yourself and believe in yourself. And you do that by telling yourself you can do it. It is part of raising your vibration. The more negative energy you remove from the conscious and the subconscious mind, the more your vibration rises automatically. With the rising of the vibration comes the knowing of universal truth and the comprehension of universal truths because then your vibration matches a vibration of knowledge and wisdom.

Embrace that part of you that is your sexual nature, your sexual aspects, and love it. It is a tool and aspect of life. It is not to be denied, controlled or manipulated, for indeed, that is what will return back to you. Love the totality of the self. The Universe does not judge. It never has. Judgment is a condition of the human mind that believes in separation and the denial of true joy.

Do not judge sexuality, whether it is heterosexual, homosexual, or bisexual. Judge it not. There is already enough hate and judgment in your world. It has saddened the Universe. Do not add to it by judging others and the methods they choose to love. Be thankful they are loving. Be thankful to yourself that you have the ability to love. Be thankful to yourself that you have the ability to accept life and be a part of life. My friends, rejoice in life. It is a grand adventure.

9

Human Relationships

This next message is to assist the human consciousness in understanding the God-within and how to express it in human relationships. The expression of the God-within between a man and a woman, between adults and their children, the God-power, or the inner knowing, has been so negated and forgotten. It is not being utilized by many on your physical Earth. Much unnecessary pain and trauma exist on your Earth because of man's inhumanity to man, brother against brother, sister against sister, man against woman, and woman against man.

We bring a teaching of simplicity, a teaching of unconditional loving. We bring a teaching of what the ego is and is not. The ego so often blocks the inner knowing, the inner development, and the inner expression. As you look about your world at the many customs that exist in your societies, notice the customs which are created by the forms of government and by your forms of religion. Customs are an invention of man. They are handed down from generation to generation and never questioned.

One such custom is the tradition that the child is inferior, that the child should automatically have great respect for adults. Yet the adults do not understand what respect is! Another such tradition in your society is where the female is considered inferior to the male. The traditions in your society dictate that the physical father must teach the physical son to be the great masculine image, to project control, and to project manipulation. Such programming within your societal traditions continues without much questioning. Such programming creates a blockage, a blockage of loving, of sharing, of learning, and of recognizing equality.

In the beginning of this particular culture in the United States (which is not united, but was given that label), the family, or the family unit, was greatly valued. Yet even during the time of your country's origin, there existed in the physical family unit a strong ego within the male form that sought to control and manipulate the female form as an inferior species. They brought forth physical children into this world, mostly to use as workers. It is important to recognize that although from generation to generation this stage of consciousness has changed in its perspectives and outlook, in how it is perceived on the outer level, the energy is still the same.

To create harmony in the family unit is to recognize that each person within the physical family is an equal. This is the first step to understand. This is the first step to begin removing the blockages. And it is important for the male to understand the need to bring forth harmony between the male and female aspects within himself. It is important for the male mind to learn to become receptive, which is a feminine aspect. Allowing this energy to be projected into the family unit would be the starting point of allowing harmony between the male and female.

It is also important for the female to allow the male aspect to come into harmony with herself. This too would create harmony within the family unit. Do this without allowing the great egos to dominate, without thinking, "I must be the great bread winner while the other is but a mate."

Such are the teachings of your great traditions. And it is these traditions which have created disharmony, pain, sorrow, and lack of loving and compassion. In order to understand the level of consciousness that exists in your culture, in your country, you must understand its origins. You need to understand the consciousness you are working with and the consciousness you were programmed with as a child.

It is first necessary to understand it, then to change it. Simply because society mandates a certain mode of living does not mean one must follow this in order to be in harmony with society, especially when society is not in harmony with the God-within. There are such contradictions within your traditions of love, marriage, and rearing children.

These latter words are merely concepts in your traditions. You do not "rear" a child, for example. You need to allow a child to develop, to grow uninhibited. To begin to understand the relationship that exists, stand back and look at the energies of each one in the physical family unit that have been projected, and ask why. How many times did the physical parents hold guilt over their children? How many times were anger and judgment projected between the male and the female in front of the children, teaching the child mind that this is how you communicate? Then, when the child has learned this, and communicates in a likewise manner to the parents, the parents cannot understand what is wrong with the child!

The consciousness of the children is a direct reflection of the consciousness of the parents. Yet often times the parents refuse to take responsibility for what they teach their children. Often times, the parents are not even consciously aware of what they are teaching the children. As one parent judges and condemns the other parent, do you expect the children to learn loving?

Recognize the family units that have been dissolved, where the husband and wife are not husband and wife any longer, and where the children live with one of the parents. Consider the difficulties that existed between the husband and wife, the judgment and anger, and the words that were spoken, if not to the children, then around the children. Consider how they began programming the consciousness of the child into disharmony and judgment of who can be loved and who cannot, who can be trusted and who cannot.

This programming within the child continues, and becomes programmed into the child's children, in a future time frame. Then you continue to have brother against brother and neighbor against neighbor because of the stipulations dictated on who should or should not be loved, who is worthy of being loved, and who is worthy of being judged.

Again, think back in your mind of the traditions created during the beginning years of the creation of this nation, when the family lived in separation. The religion taught separation between the quality of the male and female. This was enacted in the living situation of the physical family and was programmed into the children. And the children programmed this into their children.

It is beginning to shift. Many call it women's liberation. Yet even within this movement there is judgment and anger that has been repressed for many generations. And how can one act of negativity resolve the act of another's negativity?

An understanding is greatly needed in your society of taking personal responsibility. Also needed is the recognition that all are equal. But before one can recognize that all are equal, one must come into the individual personal understanding of one's own self, that he or she is an equal, to know this, to believe this, and to accept this, not from the aspect of the ego, but from the aspect of learning to love one's own self.

How can unconditional love be taught in a family, between the adults, and between the adults and the children, when the adults do not yet love their own selves unconditionally? There are always stipulations. There are always excuses. There is always such reasoning in the mind, and mental analyzing. Everyone always has a reason why he or she cannot love, why he or she must judge another, why he or she must judge the growth of another, or the lack of growth of another.

Recognize that not only are the spoken words of judgment, anger, and separation programmed into the mind of the children, but also the energy of thought, of words that are not spoken but are simply thought, thoughts that carry the energy of anger and discord that exist in the home. These are absorbed by the subconscious of the children which will in turn be projected through their consciousness according to their activities. Now is the time to begin recognizing each and every day what was programmed into the consciousness of the children.

The adults also need to reprogram what they were taught as a child. It is time to take personal responsibility for each and every thought, for each and every word you speak. Now is the time to take this responsibility in totality, not just with children but with the mate. It is not a method that is accomplished instantly. Recognize the many years it took to program the conscious mind with its traditions. And recognize that you as an individual have the ability to reprogram, restructure the energy you allow to enter into the mind.

Peace will not exist on your Earth until individual peace is accepted within yourself. And you cannot have individual peace within yourself when you hold judgments of one another or when you state that the ex-husband deserves this and that, the ex-wife deserves this and that, he or she is no good, he or she does not deserve to be loved, that he or she deserves to be punished or condemned. With this attitude of mind, you are teaching the children of your Earth to follow in your footsteps, to separate and divide. You are teaching, "This one can be loved. This one must be judged. This one, we'll think about."

So many humans cry for peace. So many cry asking for love to exist. Yet how many take the individual responsibility to begin allowing this to exist in their own personal life? How many teach this daily to their own children? How many desire their children to live in a world of peace and also teach the children peace? Do you desire children to live in a world where nations are in harmony with other nations? Do you desire that there would be no more wars? Then, teach the children to come into harmony with the next door neighbor! Also recognize, that by teaching and training the consciousness of the child you are also teaching and reprogramming your own consciousness by taking this responsibility.

To accept loving, one must first accept the individual inner loving. And when we speak of unconditional loving, which is the Christ energy, we are not speaking of sexuality, or fond embracing. Unconditional loving is recognizing equality among all. Unconditional loving is not judging your neighbor. We are not stating that you must like the negative creations your neighbors may create. But when you judge their negative creations, you are creating a negative creation yourself. To allow harmony to exist is to believe in harmony within the individual self, the individual loving. We will speak much on the subject of loving because loving is the greatest creative power.

Several decades ago (the sixties), within your society there were many running up and down the streets speaking of love, saying that all you needed to do was to sit down and love, or lay down and love, and all the problems would dissipate. The youth of that particular generation was so angered by the rigidity of the adult consciousness, and the rigid form, rules, and regulations of religion, they became fearful of what society was becoming. They began a change in the consciousness. What they neglected to see was that in addition to rejecting the old traditions, they needed to take the responsibility individually to begin creating. But so many negated their responsibility. They felt that all they needed to do was sit back and love.

They created such turmoil. The difficulty also occurred because by holding such anger and judgment against the rigid traditions, they only added to the negativity. So many wanted to escape the reality of that generation that they turned to the use of chemical drugs. They desired to alter the mind in order to escape because they were not willing to take their individual responsibility.

When we speak of love, we are not speaking of this style of love. We are speaking of a love of gentleness and meekness. We are speaking of a love of service, and of releasing the ego. We are not speaking of holding in the conscious mind that you will only do something if you get to keep something in return. What is the purpose of doing this? Of what value is growth created in this way?

We spoke earlier of marriage, and of the husband and wife. When we utilize the word "marriage" we are not speaking of a piece of paper that is a license to begin loving. A true marriage is a marriage of the heart, regardless of a piece of paper. It is an equal loving relationship, unconditionally. It is not where one is the great boss over another. It is a marriage of the heart.

Yet we find within your society so many who are entrapped because of a piece of paper, so many who live in bondage, sorrow, and pain because of what is written on a piece of paper. Is it not time to begin loving yourself enough to release yourself from bondage? Do you think another will do it for you?

You must take the individual responsibility, not in anger, not in judgment, not in condemnation, but in simply taking the responsibility that you are worthy to be loved, that you are worthy to be respected. How can you be respected when you do not respect yourself? How can you be loved when you do not love yourself? How can you teach the consciousness of children what marriage is when they see a husband and wife living in such turmoil, anger, and frustration, out of guilt because of what is written on a piece of paper?

Do you desire to see your children growing into adults and entering into a marriage controlled by a piece of paper simply because society states that you must be married? How many truly desire to see their children live the way you are living, living in so much fear and negation because you were taught as a child that this is the way it is?

Is it not time to begin questioning the traditions of your religion, the traditions of your government, and the traditions of your society, instead of sitting back and taking it at face value? Is it not time to question this? Not to judge it, but to question it. Is it loving? Is it loving when a religion dictates that the male is the head of the household? Is the wife really to be in submission to the husband? Is it not time to question this tradition that destroys the equality of living and loving? Is it not time to question what society dictates as right and wrong, and what society calls child rearing? Is it not time to question the equal rights of children? Is it not time to begin looking and searching for growth and understanding that children are souls also?

Begin recognizing each one in the family as a friend. How many husbands look at their wives as friends? How many wives look at their husbands as friends? How many fathers look at their children as friends? How many mothers look at their children as friends?

Study the old state of consciousness that told you as a child to obey every word the parent dictated. How many perceive their children as slaves? How many parents refuse to give responsibility to their children so their children may learn what responsibility is? How many parents listen to the wisdom of their children? So often times the great ego interferes and asks, "How can a child understand more than I?" So many forget to recognize that within each child's body exists a soul who has wisdom and understanding.

Recognize the stages of growth and development of the human consciousness, of the child consciousness. Take a moment to look at the age of two, for example. Your child psychologists call this the terrible twos because of the difficulties with children at this age. Difficulties exist to a greater degree at this age because this is the stage that the consciousness begins accepting a reality beyond that of the soul. This is when the battle begins occurring between unconditional loving and judgment. It is this stage of development within the child's mind that begins separating, that begins absorbing to a greater degree the judgments of the parents. At this stage is when a child is taught in accordance to society.

Recognize that children of all ages have the ability to reprogram their minds. Because you were taught by your parents certain traditions, you hold tightly in the subconscious, "It must be followed because it was taught by an authority."

There is a fear in releasing this old state of consciousness. There is also much fear in the adult mind of what the child represents. Think of the child abuse which occurs in your nation, which is occurring to such a greater degree in this time frame in this culture. It has occurred since the time of Atlantis. So many souls who were highly evolved in wisdom and understanding are choosing to incarnate, and this energy is creating fear within the rigidity of the adult consciousness. Many retaliate this fear with physical abuse, mental abuse, and sexual abuse because the adult mind has been programmed to be rigid and judgmental. The adult mind has been programmed, "Don't ask questions. Simply follow the orders."

How many of your religions teach this? How many say, "Don't ask questions—just follow the doctrine"? Many voice concern with activities in many other nations, with man's inhumanity to man.

Is it not time to recognize man's inhumanity to the children that is occurring in this nation? Is it not time to begin standing up and speaking? Is it not time to begin taking notice of the great negativity being projected and taught to the children of your nation? Is it not time for many to come out of the closet, so to speak, and begin taking responsibility for their own actions as well as assisting others who are abusing the children of your nation?

It is not just the parents who are abusing the children. Recognize the religions that hold to their old traditions that are abusing the children. Recognize the school systems that are abusing the children, if not physically, then mentally, by teaching the children to completely analyze spirituality out of life. They teach the children to live in a pure mental state of separation.

We spoke earlier of the God-within. The God-within is the life-force within each and every one. Tap into this life-force. Take responsibility for this life-force and use it. To use it is to stop mentally analyzing what life is.

To use it is to quiet the mind and to converse with your own self. To use it is to love it. To love it is to use it.

Each one has the ability and power within to love and to teach loving. Is it not time to question the educational structures of your society, from the preschools to the colleges and universities? Is it not time to begin speaking of the need for these institutions to begin teaching what life is, not teaching merely how to survive, but how to live? But as parents, do not perceive this is the school's responsibility. The main responsibility lies with the parents to teach and educate. The parents need not teach just how to survive, but how to live, how to laugh, and how to play.

Picture in your mind a world of laughter, lovingness, and playfulness. Picture a world where children of each nation are loving and respecting each other, not sitting at the great tables planning the wars because of human greed and ego. Imagine a world filled with children who do not believe in war. Imagine a world with children who do not believe in hate. Imagine a world with children who do not fall into the traps of religion that teach separation and judgment, of one religion greater than another. Imagine a world of peace.

When you can imagine this, you can achieve this. For, the children of today are the adults of tomorrow. And when the children of today are taught this, and they are taught about the God-within and the principles of the universal laws, then you shall have a world of peace. You shall have a world where negativity is rejected, not ignored, but rejected as a part of their consciousness, as a part of their illusion. You will then have a world that lives in peace.

But if you continue living in separation and in judgment of those within the family, if you continue teaching the children to judge the other parent, to judge the child next door, to judge one religion and accept another, and to judge one nation and accept another, then your world will separate and divide mentally, spiritually, and physically.

The cleansing of the darkened consciousness that exists in human relationships must first start within the individual. Unconditional loving must start by loving the self. To cease judgment one must start by ceasing judgment of one's own self. Learning to love without guilt, control, and manipulation is learning to love unconditionally. Allow truth to prevail. Give the children the opportunity to speak their wisdom.

Begin questioning your society and your religion, not in judgment or anger, but questioning what you have been programmed to believe from childhood. Question your relationships. Question why you are involved in the relationship. Is it to be an equal? Is it for sharing? Laughing? Playing? Or is it simply for economic survival? Is the relationship in existence because you each fear equally? Is the relationship in existence because you are seeking to learn from one another how to love, how to laugh, and how to play?

To end man's inhumanity to man, what must come is man's unconditional loving of man, and man's unconditional loving of the children.

10

A.I.D.S.

This chapter is about what medical science calls A.I.D.S., or what certain aspects of Christianity would call God's punishment on the sinners. There will come a day when mankind will truly learn what sin is. Sin is the transgression of one's inner being and heart. It is when one negates one's own inner being, one's own inner knowing, when one truly negates the Christ essence, which is unconditional loving. When one negates this, this is sin.

Many souls who choose to incarnate on this physical Earth choose different levels of learning, different levels of creating. When souls choose to create from the heart, and so choose their expression of loving, who has the authority to judge and condemn them? Sexuality is simply an expression of loving. When those involved in sexuality are simply choosing to express unconditional loving, one unto another, who is to stand in judgment of how it is accomplished? We are not speaking of when one seeks to force sexuality upon another. That is taking away free-will choice. What we are speaking of is when two souls choose to express loving in a sexual nature equally, one to another.

This disease called A.I.D.S. has created much fear in the mass consciousness. An understanding is needed of why the fear exists and how the medical profession, the scientists of your society, has said in the past that the majority of those affected with this disease were homosexuals. Some of Christianity has claimed A.I.D.S. is a judgment of God on the sinners. When one truly accepts the God within oneself, one can truly see the hypocrisy of such a claim.

Those who perceive themselves in the great masculine image of your society, who sit in judgment, and who fear to even speak to a person who carries A.I.D.S., will themselves create the disease. Truly, the disease has nothing to do with sexuality. But in the beginning, when medical science began perceiving there was such a disease, your scientists taught, wrote, and preached that the majority of persons having A.I.D.S. were homosexual, particularly male homosexuals.

When this disease was spoken of in the medical field, the primary focus was on homosexuals. It created much fear in the minds of those who would label themselves as homosexual. Those of this persuasion, or soul choice, were running about with such fear that they actually attracted a disease within their own physical body. They created a disease to prove to their conscious and subconscious mind their own guilt of their own sexual behavior.

A.I.D.S. is curable. There is a cure for A.I.D.S., just as there is a cause for A.I.D.S.. You create it. Just as there is a cure for cancer, there is a cure for diabetes, and there is a cure for heart disease. There is not one disease on this Earth that is incurable. But understanding this directly correlates to what and who is perceived in the mind as the authority, and what is and is not perceived as curable.

A.I.D.S. is simply an aspect of the body making a decision not to defend itself against the thoughts created in this world of condemnation and punishment. There are those who make a decision (and we are not speaking here of a conscious decision) that they need to be punished because they have listened to the doctrine of sin. Consciously, many may make the statement that they do not believe in what fundamentalist Christianity teaches, but they have accepted and absorbed this level of consciousness of condemnation, judgment, and punishment on a subconscious level.

The mind is an energy field. When the mind chooses to make a decision which directly disregards the inner being, the heart, the soul, and the

God essence, the mind attracts a level of energy of the world conscious-ness. We would describe it as a level of energy or a level of consciousness which sits in the negation of God.

Thought is energy. All thoughts that have ever been thought, that have ever been created, that have ever been expressed since your Earth has been in existence, are still in the mass consciousness. When one chooses not to take responsibility for one's own inner knowing, the mind attaches itself to what would be perceived as a bank of thoughts where many have deposited their thoughts. The person begins to believe he or she is bad, even though on a conscious level that person is making the statement he or she does not believe in a god who would burn his children or believe in a god who would sit in judgment of his own children.

Subconsciously that person has absorbed this energy of the mass con-sciousness, or a bank of thoughts, because the conscious mind, the subcon-scious mind, and/or the soul has accepted this bank of thoughts, or energy, which dictates what is right and what is wrong for everyone. The person accepts the idea that everyone must follow this prescribed set of rules. If everyone does not follow the rules, then judgment is placed on that per-son. And when judgment is placed upon someone, it is absorbed con-sciously or subconsciously. This then creates in the physical body a projection of punishment, where every cell of the body exists with the belief it needs to be punished.

The attitude one chooses from the mass consciousness is in direct corre-lation with the physical disease created to manifest one's own thoughts. In this way the Earth is unique throughout the many universes. It is not the only one like this. But it is unique in that thought forms on this Earth, conscious, subconscious, or from the soul light, create in physical matter in such a way that one creates and lives one's creation. One exists in one's creation, and one develops one's creation. And when one chooses a cre-ation of judgment, pain or condemnation, then it would become so, even though consciously one does not wish one's body to be in pain.

This disease you call A.I.D.S. is like a combination and general description of all diseases. Thought forms are beginning to manifest in this particular society, as they did in the society of Atlantis, where there also existed the disease you call A.I.D.S.. At that time, it was not labeled with this word, but it was the same disease. It was a disease that condemned different aspects of the body, just as A.I.D.S. can affect many different organs or parts of the body. As one can have A.I.D.S affecting one particular part of the body, another may have A.I.D.S. affecting a different part of the body. The part of the body this particular disease affects is the state of consciousness one has chosen from the mass consciousness.

Many speak of good and evil. Many perceive that they can establish who is right and who is wrong. But keep in mind a universal principle of the energies of positive and negative: when one chooses a negativity (and we are speaking here of negative thought forms), one is also making the decision to destroy the physical form because one is sitting in judgment of one's own creation. When one sits in judgment of what one creates, the next step within the evolutionary process is the destruction of what one has created.

There was one in your society who was known as an actor. His name was Rock Hudson. He portrayed an illusion of who he was. Although he is no longer portraying an illusion, he knew what he was. He was one who simply wanted to express kindness, gentleness, and lovingness to other souls, regardless of the form they carried, the form you call male and female.

This particular soul was a master. And let this be known to the ones who would sit in judgment of what a master is. A master is not one who follows the rules and regulations of your society. When this one was still in the physical, he spoke to the mass consciousness about who he was, and what he was. And he made the plea, "Come to understand what this disease is. Come to understand it."

This one's conscious mind lived in much fear of how he was to express his loving to another soul. Yet this one, as a soul, came to teach. He came to teach that it is not important how you love, or whom you love, but that you love. This soul, who was known in the physical as an actor, portrayed a role to humanity. This one's teaching from the consciousness was to come to understand this disease, not just to understand the medical aspects of how it is brought into the body and destroys the body, but to understand in the mind that A.I.D.S. does not need to be accepted. It does not need to be endured.

There is no need for souls to incarnate to live in pain, punishment, and suffering. That is a misconception of your societies, both east and west. There is such a thing as karma, yes. But when one can learn to accept their own Christ-beingness, not outside of themselves, but in themselves, then one learns to love unconditionally, without the great ifs and buts, such words having been created for those who wonder who they are.

When one truly understands what loving is and expresses it, there is no negative karma. When one simply makes the decision to love oneself unconditionally, then all karma of negativity, regardless of the amount of lifetimes, is instantly resolved.

This master, who was in the physical, resolved the karma, the karma he created in his life of living in such fear of what ones would think of whom he loved. If those of the great self-righteousness, who would condemn how this one loved, could only step aside and love themselves to the same degree, then there would not be such disharmony, such pain, and such fear projecting in your society.

So many use the book you call the Bible as the book of rules to judge by. If only you would understand the original manuscripts of this book before they were altered by the mind of mankind that chose to live in judgment, that chose to establish rules and regulations of how to live and how to love! If only you would come to allow the mind to accept the teachings of the master Jesus, who was truly called Jeshua, or to accept the teachings of the master Muhammad, or the master Buddha, or of any master that existed. They were all the same teachings. There is no difference.

The difference lies in the interpretations of the small minds that would dictate right and wrong, good and evil. Truth is so simple. However, if we were to speak on an intellectual level, those of the great complicated minds would perceive they are truly hearing an intellectual message. We refuse to do this because universal truths are so simple. Truly, the answer to all difficulties is the same, even though some may state there are difficulties greater than others. Some people's difficulties are greater than others only because they have worked at it longer!

Those who carry this disease called A.I.D.S., those who would be of the persuasion called homosexuality, need to learn to meditate, which is simply quieting the mind. Journey in time, in this lifetime, back to the age when you, as a conscious being, recognized the sexual persuasion so chosen as an expression of loving. Envision yourself at that age, and begin speaking to this visionary being of yourself in the physical. Teach this being it is not important how you love. What is important is that you do love. Teach this being in the physical, who is yourself, to reject consciously and subconsciously all judgments of society, parents, friends, and relatives. Know that you know you are guilty of nothing.

It is so ironic that your society, which is in a world so void of loving, sits in judgment of whom one loves instead of praising the soul essence, the God essence, and Christ essence, instead of praising the fact that at least one is loving, regardless of whether one is homosexual, heterosexual, or bisexual. The process of loving is the same for all.

So many speak of the Christ. But so many speak of the Christ in a negative aspect. They use the word "Christ" as their tool of judgment and condemnation, instead of recognizing that this entity simply represents unconditional loving.

Those of you who fear contracting this disease called A.I.D.S., ask yourself why you fear it. Do you fear it because you believe you are doing something bad? Are you living in judgment of how you love, of how you must choose so many multiple partners because if you chose only one, and it was male with male, or female with female, you would run the risk of being found out? Therefore, the mind would analyze that you must choose multiple partners for one or two days, one or two weeks, or one or two months because of your own great fear that someone in society may know how you are loving, that society would be greatly concerned about whom you are loving.

How many people are living in pain, experiencing wars, famines, and diseases in what you would call your third world nations, who also exist in the United States as the oppressed? Those who are oppressed have chosen to be oppressed and are also choosing to make a statement of what equality is. So many give such concern, such judgment, of what is good and evil. Know that no one needs to carry A.I.D.S.

We ask you not to just read this message. We ask you to live this message. We ask no one to follow us. We ask no one to walk in front of us. But we ask all of you to walk beside us, in a march of truth. For, the mind of mankind which lives in such judgment, which has imprisoned its own beingness from expressing loving, let this message be shared and spoken of openly. You do not need to take a friend into a private room to tell him or her you read the message because of fear that you may be judged by someone else. What is the difference? That you fear you might be judged because of what you believe and what you read? Or you would be judged because of whom you love and how you love?

We will end this message with the message of the one we call the actor who played a role—come to understand the disease, and come to understand what creates it.

Come to understand yourself. Come to understand the Christ. And come to love your own beingness. Stop listening to the judgment and condemnation of your society, of your mass consciousness. Start living. Stop fearing how you are going to survive, and start living. And live with the fullness of the heart.

As we existed in the physical in the histories of your Earth, and as we taught freedom from fear, freedom from religion, and freedom from government, we will return to share and to teach the same message because mankind has the habit of forgetting truth but remembering fear.

Know, and know that you know, that you are worthy to be loved and you are worthy to be what you are, regardless of what a small mind would think.

11

Prophecy

Good day beloved ones. We seek to bring you an understanding of the word "prophecy," particularly during this time in your culture. There have been many prophecies made regarding the time coming forth. There needs to come a clarity, a much greater understanding. We find that so many are carrying intense fear of prophesies of old which relate to this day and age. What so greatly needs to be understood is that a prophecy is never an absolute. Indeed, as we have always stated, there are no absolutes that can exist. What also needs to be understood is that all of you, all of your different levels of consciousness, and all of your different levels of fear do play a direct part in what is called prophecy.

So many people have written books on this subject, about many terrifying events coming to your world. And many are holding very rigid beliefs, that there is coming an end to civilization, even an end to your planet, perhaps. Understand well that the Earth is not going to be destroyed. Civilization, humanity, is not going to come to an end. You are here as bearers of light. Many souls have come forth in physical form to project, to teach, and to assist in bringing about the Light, the Christed-consciousness.

There is a change coming to your Earth. There is a change coming to the mass consciousness of your planet, of your world. There is no end coming to the Earth. So many have been searching in the prophecies of the Hopi, the prophecies of the Mayan, the prophecies of Nostradamus, and the prophecies of the book of Revelation in your Bible. Understand, many of these prophecies have been symbolic.

Also understand that those parts of the prophecies which were not symbolic, but were meant as literal, were based on a state of mind, a state of consciousness which you would call your future of humanity, the future which is now the present. If the consciousness had not been changing, if the beings of light had not come forth, then many of these cataclysmic events would have occurred.

We would also like to bring greater clarity, particularly for you who live in the United States, regarding those predicting that half of your continent will fall into the ocean. This will not occur, be of assurance.

There will be movements of land upon the Earthquake faults in the western parts of your United States, specifically California, Washington, Alaska, and certain portions of land in Western British Columbia. Understand that this prophecy is based upon the degree of consciousness that exists at this time. There is always in existence free-will choice. And free-will choice can, does, and has changed prophecy.

The prophecies of old were made for specific reasons. They were warning messages to humanity to look at what you have been creating, to look at where you are headed, to change your thinking, to change your consciousness, to begin accepting your own Christed-consciousness, and to create a movement to what has been called a New Age, a new level of consciousness. Every two thousand years there is a change in consciousness or what could be termed a New Age. It is like an evolutionary spiral, an evolutionary process of the soul as well as the Earth, your physical planet.

These prophecies were a warning to take heed. Remain in the old ways, and the events we are speaking of will occur. Change the old ways by beginning to take total responsibility for what you are as a god, by beginning to take responsibility for what you think and what you allow to enter into the mind, by beginning to take responsibility for what you create, to allow the expression of the Christed-consciousness, which is loving yourself and all-that-is unconditionally. Do this and many of the changes in the land masses, in the water masses, will not need to occur.

But also understand that whenever there is a catastrophe where many are injured or killed, there are many in the communities and outside of the communities who come to assist in that catastrophe. Recognize how many pour their hearts out in assisting, in bringing forth foods, monies, and shelter for those involved in the catastrophe, those who lost their homes and lost members of their family. Recognize the loving energy which occurs when there is a catastrophe.

The Earth is well aware of this. When there are Earth changes, there are also dramatic shifts in consciousness and great outpourings of love unconditionally, of support, and of compassion from one to another. We are not stating that a catastrophe or movement of land mass or water mass needs to occur before an expression of the Christed-consciousness can occur. What we are seeking to teach you is to take a much greater degree of responsibility for what you are, to allow the movement and expression of your own Christed-consciousness. Then the events, such as the movement of land and water we have been speaking about, do not need to occur.

Beloved friends, you are the ones who are responsible for the outcome of the prophecies which have been given. Do not fear the prophecies of the Mayans, the Hopis, and the Bible's book of Revelation about the end of the world. Do not fear the devastation of your cities, your peoples, or your children. Do not give power to it. We are not stating not to listen to these prophesies. We are not stating this at all. What we are stating is to not give it the power of fear. It is not more powerful than you.

These prophecies of old are for a purpose. Their purpose is not to frighten or to create fear, but to create a warning. You are in the midst of a time of change. On August 17, 1987, the emotional body of the Earth shifted realities. When you have a majority of realities shifting to a higher vibration, the energy moves to another dimension. We have spoken of this dimension before. It is called the fourth dimension. Dimension is a different frequency, a different vibration of the electromagnetic energy structure of the physical essence of this planet, as well as the physical essence of body matter, called your tissue matter, as well as the essence of your spirit. These Earth changes, the diseases, the wars, are not going to occur in the fourth dimension. They were never prophesied to occur in the fourth dimension.

The fourth dimension is a physical dimension which is equal in the yin and the yang. It is a dimension of balance, and a dimension of lovingness. And you, as you raise your own vibration on your own pathways, as you continue to shift to new realities, you can move your vibration to enter into the fourth dimension.

In terms of the emotional body shifting realities, those of you who are centered in your own emotional knowing, knowing who and what you are and your purpose, will experience incredible growth, movement and tranquility. But those who continue suppressing and hiding their emotions, negating their own god selves, negating their own lives, it will be perceived as if they are being tested. It will be perceived as if they are being pushed to the limits, showing their true colors.

Do not receive this message with the fear that the bad are being punished and the good are being blessed. We are not speaking in these terms at all. All we are stating here is that those who have not built their foundation on a rock will find their foundations washed away when the storms come. Those who build their foundations on a rock, on inner knowing, on knowing in truth and totality what they are in their purpose, will weather the storms. Those who have their foundations, meaning their inner knowing and inner truth, built on a rock, built on firm support of their own spiritual beingness, will not be affected by the coming changes in your world.

Now, when we make a prophecy, we do not simply draw it out of a hat. We look at your world, at the thought forms that exist, and the thought atmosphere of your world. Just like your regular atmosphere which circles your planet, there is another atmosphere of thought form. Thoughts are projected and placed within this sphere of existence. Place a majority of negative thoughts within the thought atmosphere and you will have a negative creation. Looking at this and reading these thoughts, one can predict, or make a prophecy, of what will be occurring.

Thoughts create. Remember this always. Yet we are not just referring to what one speaks verbally, or even what one thinks.

People are going to be confronted with their own thought forms in this coming change, but not as a punishment. People must come to recognize the responsibility for what they have created. By reading and looking at these thoughts, they can then determine what these thoughts, in the etherical level, are in the process of creating.

Although many prophecies look negative, many are also positive. During what is called the New Age, there is coming a time of world peace, a time of weather being in harmony with humankind, a time when there will not be violence, wars, and diseases, and a time when the Christed-consciousness is projected in totality. This planet of yours will become like a shining star in its evolutionary spiral back to the Source, called the universal God essence. Allow your thoughts and attitudes to be directed to the positive prophecies. Do not hold on with fear of survival to negative prophecies that have been predicted, many of which will never come.

We look out to so many of you wondering how to survive, wondering if you should move here or there, wondering if you should store food, searching for a guru, an entity, or a master to follow and protect you. Do not do this out of fear. Never make a movement to another geographical location based on fear of survival. The energy you carry will be the outcome of your journey. Do not store food out of fear of starving. The Universe provides all that is necessary when you are in harmony with the Universe.

We well understand that there are many conflicting messages being projected in your culture. There are many books reflecting different levels of human consciousness. Some books are by different masters who are teaching and speaking through physical forms, some making prophecies, some not making prophecies. What is needed to be understood is that there are many different levels of consciousness which exist in your society. There is no such thing as one absolute truth. Remember this well. There is not one absolute truth. There are multiple truths for multiple levels of consciousness. That is why there are many masters coming forth to teach different levels of consciousness. Therefore, when trying to compare different messages from only one level of consciousness it can be perceived as if there are conflicting messages.

There are some masters who have come to teach what fear is. There are some masters who have come to teach what unconditional loving is. There are some masters who have come to teach what responsibility is. There are some masters who have come to teach what transmutation is. And there are some masters who have come to teach survival.

Understand that once you have learned, you do not need to re-enter into that particular school and continue learning. Regarding the subject of fear of survival, grow through it, learn through it, but do not remain in it. The teachings you receive will be greatly successful.

A prophecy is never to be taken as an absolute. Nothing is to be taken as an absolute. Allow no one to make your decisions for you. Indeed, allow yourself to be open to the Christed-consciousness and the Light. And allow yourself to be open to the teachings from many masters, but as a guidance, not as an absolute. Never make a decision based on an entity stating you must do this or you must do that. Always make your own decisions based on your inner feelings, your inner intuition, and psychic knowing.

All of you are psychic. Let no one tell you that only the privileged or gifted ones are psychic. All are psychic, although some have developed this ability more than others. Always base your decisions on your inner knowing, your inner feeling, and your inner truth. A true master will never take responsibility for you, but will teach you total and complete responsibility.

Life is to be lived with great joy and universal tranquility, not in hiding your emotions or your fears. Life is not to be lived in daily fear, wondering, "Will there be an atomic war? Will there be mass destruction and starvation?"

Do not give power to these fears. Recognize that what you fear, what you give power to, you will eventually experience. That is why we constantly teach you to be responsible for all that you allow in your mind. Be responsible for all of your thoughts. What you think, you will experience. What you believe, you will become. There is not one reality. There are multiple realities from which to experience, grow, and learn. Take heed of what you are. Recognize that you as a soul-god are equal to all that exists. Do not give your power away to society, religion, government, or the many forms of gurus. Do not give your power away. Rather, maintain your own equality and your own truth.

Always remember that what you fear, you will experience. And you do not need to experience fear to grow. Indeed not. Allow yourself to love, to continue to grow, to expand, because you are making a decision that life is worth living, that life is worth loving, and that it is time to dance and sing. It is time to play as children. It is time to put aside the fear of fear.

All of you have chosen to incarnate in a time of change, a time of movement, and a time which prophesied two thousand years ago the return of Christ, not the individual called Jeshua, but the Christed-consciousness. You have chosen to incarnate in the midst of great change. You have not come here to fear the change or to try and find out how to survive the change, but to be a part of the change.

There are so many in your world who live in daily pain, fear, disease, and separation. All of that is coming to an end. It is coming to the completion of a cycle. The cycle has been one of learning through pain, separation, and denial. That cycle is ending. Now ones will come to the Earth to learn through loving, joy, rejoicing and universal tranquility.

You are a part of that change. You are seeking your own enlightenment. You are seeking to come to know what God is, not the man-made god who judges, condemns, and seeks to punish for eternity. There is no universal god like that. But there is a united God essence of the Universe that does not judge or condemn.

When you are separated by your own denial and your own fears, then pain exists. Pain is a reminder, a reminder to stop and look at what you are doing, what you are doing to yourself, to look at the diseases you are creating because of this pain and fear, to look at the separation you are living in.

Pain is a reminder, a reminder that you are not on your inner pathway. An inner pathway is not one of pain. The inner pathway we are referring to is directly connected with your higher self, which is not in separation from the universal God essence.

Your world is a world of thought. When you do not take responsibility, those thoughts, or what is called the thought atmosphere, begins taking over your mind. It begins controlling you. And it controls based on fear. It is better known as the mass consciousness of the world mind. As you come to recognize this, as you come to recognize your own responsibility to yourself, and not to the world, you begin quieting the mind, you begin moving the mind from the beta brain waves to the delta brain waves, connecting your mind with the higher self. Your painful reality ceases to be, and the prophecies of old no longer apply to you.

To become enlightened is to come out of pain, fear, and separation. By allowing your own inner Christed-consciousness to emerge, you are ending this separation. You are stating, by the acceptance of your own Christed-consciousness, you will no longer accept pain as a reality that must be endured to create growth. Indeed, pain is a teacher, but so is true joy and universal tranquility. Which teacher do you wish to be a part of? That teacher is a part of you and it is a matter of choice. And it is never forced on you by an outside force which one to choose. It is always of your own choosing.

Your Earth is not truly solid. There are many Earths, so to state. It is like what is called a Chinese box, a dimension within a dimension, within a dimension, within a dimension. Some have prophesied that many individuals will go into the inner world to escape the cataclysms which will occur.

We would like to bring some understanding of what the inner world is. It is not what is physically inside the Earth or the core of the Earth. The inner world is of a different dimension, a different vibration and frequency. The inner world we are speaking of is inner thoughts which are equal in the yin and yang balance. The world we are referring to is called thought forms.

The Earth we are speaking of is what you perceive as your planet. Your planet is not all what you see or think it is. Those of you in this third dimension see your Earth from a third dimensional point of view. Those of you who are in the third dimension see the third dimension as physical solid substance. Because of the vibration of the electromagnetic energy field, you are seeing it through light refraction. That light refraction, from your point of consciousness, is as real to you as anything is on this physical planet Earth in the third dimension. Change the electromagnetic energy field, you also change the light refraction. And that light refraction changes what you experience and what you see. That is why we teach that what you are truly seeing out there is an illusion, and it is an illusion based upon light refraction.

There are many doorways to this inner world in many different locations on your planet. One such doorway is what is known as the Bermuda triangle. Many have gone to search the Bermuda Triangle only to find nothing abnormal. They find no doorways, and yet they cannot find the ones who are missing. That is because these doorways open and close in direct response to the sunspots on your sun. When there is activity in accordance with these sunspots, it creates a shift in your atmosphere. It creates a shift in the electromagnetic energy field. Thus, it creates a shift in light refraction, and then one enters into another dimension.

The fourth dimension is a dimension of balance. It is a physical dimension. As the energy or thought forms of your world begin shifting to a higher vibration, that energy is directly involved with the electromagnetic energy field. You can change the electromagnetic energy field by thought, and you can change the energy or the vibratory state of that thought. And when the light energy comes and creates a movement, it creates a mass opening to the fourth dimension. Those who have raised their vibration to an equal vibration of the fourth dimension will exist in the fourth dimension where there will not be cataclysms, war, or ownership.

The ownership we are speaking of here is where the male egos in your culture perceive they own the female, their children, and others. A dictatorship government perceives it owns the population. There will not be ownership. There will be an ease in totality and equality.

It is important to understand one cannot enter into the fourth dimension with the attitude and thought that one wants to enter into it to escape the third dimension. Thoughts and attitudes with the energy of escapism lower your vibration. They do not raise your vibration. Therefore, it is not as if some god is out there stating, "You and you and you and perhaps this one will be saved!" There is no savior out there coming to take you away. There is no escape. There is only resolvement, even if that resolvement takes ten thousand life times. There is not, never has been, never will be an escape, only resolvement.

There have also been predictions and prophecies made about extraterrestrials, space beings in their space ships who are coming to evacuate the good people of the Earth. There are beings from other planetary systems who visit your planet from time to time. There are ships, or what you call UFOs, but they are not unidentified. Your government knows of them and has communicated with them. But the point is that these beings and ships are not coming to take you away from the Earth because of the cataclysms of the Earth. They are not coming as a savior for you. They are not coming to take your responsibility.

There are many planetary systems with physical life. But the thoughts which are projected in the thought atmosphere create a blockage from truly seeing what is in the Universe. As these thoughts come into clarity, as the thoughts rise in vibration, there will be much more direct contact with beings from other planetary systems.

Many changes are coming. There will be certain parts of your land mass which will change, but not half of the continent falling into the ocean! A light is coming to your world, a light which was prophesied and which we still see as coming to your world, although it can be delayed by what the mass consciousness chooses to experience. But you do not need to delay yourself because of the mass consciousness delaying itself. You can raise your own vibration and move into the fourth dimension.

There are changes coming which have been prophesied by many. Do not accept any prophecy as an absolute, particularly the timing of the prophecy. Timing is chosen in direct accordance to your degree of manifestation. If we give a time frame for a certain event, and the individual or group of individuals choose to either speed their growth or delay their growth, then this will change the timing. No timing we have ever given, or ever will give, will be an absolute. Timing is based on the calculation of the degree of growth you are presently in. Maintain that degree of growth, and the timing will be accurate. Change the degree of growth, the timing will change.

You are your own creator. You are your own truth. You are your own savior. And you are responsible in totality for what you are.

As you are changing and raising your vibration, you may worry if you see around you that the world is not at the same degree you are. You may wonder if this means you will still experience certain Earth changes simply because you are in the same geographical location. The answer to that is "no," unless you fear it, unless you fear you are locked into what they have created. Then you will. If you do not fear, then you are not locked into what they have created and you can change your own reality, raise your vibration, and even move into another dimension. Because those around you choose not to change, does not mean you need to experience their experience.

Prophecy is to be looked at as a warning that this is what you are about to create if you do not change from your own fear and negativity. Prophecy can be described as a warning device to be looked at and recognized from the heart. And then a choice is to be made, a choice based on self-worth, self-loving, and self-responsibility.

Look well at prophecies, but do not fear them. They are warnings. You do not need to experience what the prophets of old have prophesied. What you need to experience is life, laughter, true joy, and universal tranquility. Remember, assistance is available to all. Ask for it and be willing to receive it. It is not there to take your responsibility, but simply to assist you as you take responsibility for yourself.

12

The New Age Unveiled

Good day friends of the Earth who enjoy nature, peace, tranquility, the simplicity of living, and the simplicity of life! As you look at the sun, recognize the life that it gives. As you look at the flow of water, recognize the life that it gives. As you listen to your wind and your air, recognize the life that it gives in this physical plane of existence.

At this time we will speak about matters of simplicity and matters of the heart. We will speak about what many are coming to recognize on your Earth as the New Age. We will speak about the coming New Age, what it is, and what it is not, how it is going to come about, and when it is going to come about. So many people, in their intellects and planning, have missed the concept of what the New Age is. Many are already trying to organize it. They are trying to create followings, groups, and organizations to build their pyramids and to find their crystals.

The New Age is much more simplistic. Many people try to hang on to this civilization's old concepts, old ideas, and old states of consciousness. They hang on so dearly and try to bring these into the New Age, simply because they do not understand what it is. They fear change. But be assured, change is coming to this Earth not too many years from now. Many changes have already begun. Many movements of consciousness have already begun.

We will speak first as to the purpose of why a New Age is coming. Why does this world need to be rejuvenated? Why does this world need to wake up out of its amnesia? Why does this world need to start looking for a simpler way of life? Rather than running about in the corporate empires you have created, learn a life of simplicity, a life of true joy, a life free from worry, a life free from pain, a life free from trauma. In this world of yours, you have worked so hard to separate and categorize truth that you have lost it. You have lost the meaning of life and the purpose of living. You are just surviving. Your world teaches you simply how to survive.

What many do not understand is that your Earth works in cycles. Some would call it evolutionary cycles of development, or movements of energy. The Earth is a school. And you have the free-will choice to choose whatever subject matter you desire in this school. There is no such thing as failure, for life is eternal. Whether one so chooses to come to this school for one incarnation and gain enlightenment or ten thousand incarnations and gain enlightenment, so be it. The Universe does not judge.

Every twenty-four thousand years there is a cycle on your Earth. There is a shift of the physical Earth plane, an expansion of land mass and water mass, a movement of the plates of the Earth. What is coming here is a coinciding of both the two thousand year cycle and the twenty-four thousand year cycle. The Earth is also an entity that has free-will choice and is experiencing its own growth, its own knowledge, its own wisdom, its own lovingness, as all of you are. What is coming is the return of the Lemurian consciousness, which was the original consciousness upon the Earth plane.

What is coming about is a teaching about how to live from the heart in simplicity. Do you listen to the birds sing? Do they run about and gather their organizations and groups to worry where the next meal is coming from? They do not worry. They simply live in harmony with nature, and with the Earth. And when you respect life, when you respect the Earth, when you love the Earth, the Earth supplies all that is needed. It is the mother of life and it teaches us balance.

Long ago, in your perception of time, there existed a land where the physical beings lived in harmony with the Earth. The Earth was a place of true joy. The Earth supplied all that was needed simply for the asking, when the asking was from the heart. It was a land of many colors. The skies held a multitude of colors, many the human eye cannot even comprehend. The water was colored. The animal kingdom lived in peace with humankind. The animals simply reflected love that was given to the Earth by the humans. There was no fear of being attacked by wild animals. There was no fear of being attacked by brothers and sisters. There was no fear of death. There was no fear of living. It was a land of true joy, of true harmony. The word "pollution" was unknown. It did not exist. Children could wander the countryside alone. They could communicate with the animals. They could communicate with the trees, with the wind, and with the water. It all holds a consciousness. It all holds knowledge because there is no separation. Only in the belief of separation has mankind lost the art of communication with the Earth.

This land was called Lemuria. Lemuria was a continent that existed in the Pacific Ocean, but it was not limited to the continent called by this name. It was a state of consciousness that existed with the Earth. It was a land in which you could create with the heart and with the mind because the mind was not separate from the heart.

There are many souls from other planetary systems. We will speak of one planet in particular, known as Maldek. It existed in the asteroid belt of your solar system. On that particular planet, an evolution of the mind was created, not an evolution of the heart. Souls from Maldek had already learned to live in separation from the God-source, from nature, from the animal kingdom, and the plant kingdom. They polluted their waters. They polluted their soils. They polluted their air. And they destroyed their physical planet.

Since life is eternal, there is no such thing as eternal death. Many of the souls from Maldek came to Earth. Certain symbologies have been written about this. There was a story of this land written in a book, yet many have not understood its symbologies, largely because the book has been greatly altered and changed. This book is called your Bible. Do you know the story of the "Garden of Eden"? Lemuria was the Garden of Eden. This was where souls began incarnating upon the Earth plane. Many souls from Maldek came to the Garden of Eden. They were not in dense form, as you see the bodies in this time. It was more as an etherical body, a higher vibration of energy. There was not the separation of male and female, but rather, forms were androgynous.

Through many thousands of years through the incarnating in this form upon the Earth plane, the souls that began creating upon the Earth plane began allowing their own creations to control them, to manipulate them, much like what occurs in your world at the present time, but to a different degree. How often do you create your own creation, then you perceive you are controlled by what you have created? You perceive you have become lost in what you have created—when all one needs to do is come to understand you are your own god and you have your own power to change your creation, that no one needs to be a slave to the world mind, or a slave to the social consciousness.

Indeed, the energy of the Lemurian continent became dense. As many souls began losing sight that they were God, they began separating that of their own aspect, of male/female, perceiving they could create more, and became more lost in their creation. The forms that began taking form, of a male body, and a female body, over what you would term a period of time, is the story of "Adam and Eve." And in that story, was not Eve taken from the rib of Adam? The true meaning of the story was the separation of the male and female aspects, that indeed, they began placing their own godship, their own power outside of themselves. Kicked out of the Garden of Eden by a god? No, by themselves! The original sin, written in symbolic terms, was the separation of the mind from the heart.

Many of these souls (from Maldek) began bringing their knowledge of separation to this Earth. They began creating separation with the mind, and the animal kingdom rebelled. It became wild. The Earth began rebelling. There occurred many upheavals in the land, such as volcanoes, earthquakes, hurricanes, and tidal waves, because the Earth was rebelling. Thus, the continent of Lemuria physically sank, not all at once, but over a period of 250,000 years. It began crumbling. It became disorganized. The human minds lost their perception of how to live. Those souls only looked at how to survive.

We, the Jonah, the Teacher of Righteousness, assisted in bringing light into Maldek. Many souls who have chosen to walk with us in the physical are also soul beings who assisted in bringing light into Maldek. The light was rejected. The planet dissolved. We came forth again to Lemuria to assist in awakening the mind to what the heart is. Many chose not to listen. Many chose to stay in the intellect and to only give credit to a world of separation. They looked to the world as their savior. They looked to the world for their survival.

Thus was the creation of what many of you know as Atlantis. It was a continent that existed in what you now call the Atlantic Ocean. Those who lived physically in Lemuria, when it began separating and crumbling, found new lands to inhabit. Not all the people in Lemuria became greatly mental, although many did. And those who became greatly mental chose the continent of Atlantis because of the minerals and Earth there, which they perceived would give them power. Because of the boundaries of oceans on the Atlantean continent, they perceived they could wage great wars and yet be protected. They chose it out of their minds. They took from the Earth what was not truly theirs.

Atlantis became a strong nation. It developed scientists and astronauts. The people of Atlantis highly developed their crystals, which, after a period of time, they began worshipping. They took the power of the mind and put it within a crystal to worship. They worshipped power, they worshipped the ego, they worshipped one another. It was the origination of what would be termed the worshipping of a god outside of themselves. What has been discussed in your religious histories as pagans who worship idols, this was the origination of the concept to begin worshipping either an entity, a deity, an object, a rock, or a statue. This concept began in Atlantis, but not as a form of religion.

Religion was created when more complicated mental attitudes began. Atlantis began creating images, illusions, environments outside of themselves. Many in Atlantis began perceiving the great almighty power was within a crystal. But not at first. At first, they began understanding the composition of a crystal, the molecules of a crystal, that it was a transmitter and receiver of energies, which it is.

Ones began worshipping, thinking a crystal would protect them, a crystal would heal them, a crystal would save them. There was created a crystal, that even unto this time there has not been created a crystal of its size. It was placed within a city called Adona. Ones from all across the lands journeyed as pilgrims to ask for blessings from this crystal, to ask for healings from this crystal, to ask for miracles from this crystal. Some of them received it (a miracle), but not from the crystal. They received it from their own belief the crystal would give it.

The Atlanteans perceived themselves as a highly evolved society that nothing could stop. They developed what is called flight in their machines, not the same as what you have in this time frame with the fuels. They learned the energies of the Earth. They understood the atom and how to separate it. They understood the concept of the mind, of how to control and manipulate through fear.

There came a leader of the land, who called himself an emperor. To prove the loyalty to the emperor, you had to worship the crystal, which was referred to as the god of all that existed. There were truly energies and powers within this crystal.

There also existed in this culture which worshipped this particular crystal, the ownership of others, slaves. The emperor taught that there were different classes of what existed. There was a supreme class, middle class, and lower class, which is much of what you see in this society today in accordance to the mental concepts that exist. The people had to swear their allegiance to their culture, to their emperor. To be a scientist, to be one who truly was searching of the energies, one had to be willing to give one's power away, one had to have their permission, one could not cross the taboos of the land.

For many centuries their minds created destruction on Atlantis. They warred against many peoples of the Earth who were choosing to live in simplicity. They were known as the warriors of the world. They took pride in their battlefields. They took pride in how many they could murder. Their aim was to conquer the world.

They did not succeed because the world that they knew began crumbling. Again, the Earth began breaking apart and crumbling. Again, there were eruptions of volcanoes. The plates of the Earth began moving. There were the tidal waves and hurricanes, not all at once, but over a period of time.

Atlantis sank to the floor of the ocean. It sank under the seas because the powers, the energies of the Earth they utilized, rebelled. The continent ceased to exist. The consciousness did not, just as you see many forms of government in your current world, the many forms of religion, each claiming they are superior. To what? "They" have the answer. To what?

There are still remnants of Atlantis on the floor of the ocean. It is only the mental skeptics who do not wish to search it. But it still exists, nonetheless.

Many of the ones who turned to the heart, because they saw what the mind separated from the heart was doing, established colonies in many locations throughout the Earth. Many went to the location of Egypt. Many went to what you call Ancient Greece. Many went to the Southwest of your United States. They went in order to depart from the mind and to learn what the heart is. They were learning again to turn back to nature, to allow nature to supply life, to supply the true joy of living, and to heal their bodies.

For many in Atlantis there was an epidemic of what you have come to know as cancer, leprosy, and brain tumors. They were quite common. This was not because of what people put into their bodies physically. It was the thoughts people put into their minds which destroyed the body, just as thoughts are now destroying the Earth.

You see, your body is made up of all the minerals of the Earth. Your physical body, the vehicle in which you carry a soul, is not truly separated from the Earth. Every mineral you can find in the body exists in the Earth. It is Mother Earth who is the giver of life to the physical form.

We have seen two large powerful cultures crumble because of the mind living in separation. What you are now seeing in this culture, in this world, is a nation at war, one nation battling another nation with their invisible boundaries, brother killing brother, and sister killing sister. Corporations of your society are polluting your Earth out of greed for profits, for monies. Again, your Earth is rebelling. Again, your volcanoes, your hurricanes, and your coast lands are crumbling into the ocean because the mind still refuses to look at the heart. The mind still refuses to look at the simplicity of nature.

Many of your waters hold chemicals which can destroy a physical body. You have created and placed many gasses into your atmosphere. You have created an imbalance in nature. You use the waters as your sewers and you use the skies in the heavens as your garbage dumps because you fear not surviving. You must have the money. You must have the profits. You do not give credit to the God-source, the creative source of the Universe. You simply give credit to the mind.

Many of the lands on your Earth will crumble. Many will sink. Your governments, as you see them, will perish. All that exists which is not in harmony will perish. This destruction and reality is already being created.

Did you know that the Hawaiian Islands were the mountain tops of Lemuria? The shifts that will take place on your Earth will not destroy these, but rather there will be added islands in this location. In addition, center portions of the coast of the state you call Oregon, and Washington state, and that of the Canadian coast, and the Alaskan Coast, part of this is part of the ancient land mass of what was called Lemuria. There will be land masses rising up out of the water between the location of the center of Oregon state to what is called the Aleutian Islands. There will be created as great lakes, similar to what is already in your country, between this land mass and the Washington coast.

In what you perceive as your West, south of this location, there will be movement of land. The fault line which lies in Washington state, that travels through the Seattle location to the Aleutian Islands, there will be a shift, a movement of the land mass moving northward from the fault line to the coast. This area will begin moving, as it already is. But it will move in a more rapid degree to the north.

There will be movements of land in what you would call the Mississippi Valley, of which there exists under the land surface many old and ancient caverns that have been filled with fluids. There has been the constant removal of the fluids, which will create the collapse of these caverns, of much land mass in this area. There has already been movement of this.

Your weather will begin changing, even as you presently see it already beginning to occur. The poles of your Earth are wobbling on their axis and it is increasing. It has created a movement of the jet stream that creates a shift in your weathers. There is needed a movement in your weather to cleanse that which is in the jet stream, to cleanse many of the toxins and the chemicals that continue poisoning your land, your plants, the animal kingdom, and the human kingdom. You will see more of this occurring.

But it is not our purpose here to dwell upon the negative aspects of the pain which will be created because mankind has negated the heart. It is our purpose to describe in detail what is coming after this. There is a new world coming that would be forced on no one. But indeed, the new world will embrace all who desire it. And there is not required a belief in it for the New Age to come forth.

What is the New Age, my friends? It is the return, the return to what you truly are, the return of the Christ, which has been misinterpreted by your religions as an entity called Jesus returning to save you. The return of the Christ will occur. But it is a state of consciousness. It is a state of being. It is a state of loving. It is a state of taking total responsibility for whom and what you are. It is a return of the Lemurian state of consciousness. It is the completion, my friends, of a cycle.

The waters will be purified, the airs will be purified, the soils will be purified, and mankind will learn to live in balance with the Earth. This Earth will not be destroyed, as Maldek was. It will not be destroyed. You will not have the total nuclear destruction which so many on your Earth fear. This will not occur. It will be prevented, although not by mankind. It will be prevented by many brotherhoods from many universes in order to keep and return to harmony.

Again, we have come to your Earth for a time to teach what the mind is and what the heart is, and to assist mankind again to come into balance. We have come to teach you that you do not need to worship a religion or a corporation, and there is not much difference between these. We have come to teach you to worship your own heart, to begin worshipping the Earth and the God-force, not to worship a man, nor to worship us. We do not allow it. Worship harmony and simplicity.

Many of you take the wrong meaning of the word "worship." Worship simply means to give credit to, to give life substance to, to give honor to. We are speaking here in the sense of worshipping the Earth, loving the Earth, loving your brothers and sisters, loving your children and parents, and loving your neighbors.

A protective shield used to exist in your Earth. Much of the moisture in your atmosphere was held within this protective shield. You did not have the great extremes in temperature as you now do in the North and South Poles, and in the Equator. You did not have the great barren deserts like the Sahara. There were no droughts. These extremes are simply created because of the imbalance of nature, what the mind has created on this Earth.

There will come a time when this Earth will physically tilt 17 degrees on its axis. When this occurs, there will come a great light from the skies which will be able to be seen from every location on Earth. It will be an energy field directed to this planet by a universal source of energy. It will be an energy of total unconditional loving, not just for mankind, but for the planet Earth. This energy shield will neutralize all toxins and poisons in the soil, the waters, and the skies.

There again will be a shield around this Earth, like a bubble. There will be much moisture in the atmosphere. There will not be sudden spells of dry air or downstreams of rain that creates floods and carries the topsoils to the floor of the ocean. There will again be brilliant colors in your skies and in your waters. There will be no separation between nation and nation. There will be no artificial boundaries of your nations. There will be no governments that seek to control, manipulate, and deny life.

Freedom will not be denied! Freedom will be an expression in every location on the Earth. Mankind again will look to the physical substance of the Earth, knowing that it simply needs to ask for the physical food substance, and the Earth will freely give it.

The energy of creativity will abound. There will be technology, but it will be in balance with nature. It will use the energy from the sun. It will not burn the oils from the Earth, which lubricate the plates, thus polluting the air. You will be able to drink from all the waters in the Earth. You will not have to place chemicals in the water so that people think it is safe to drink! Placing chemicals in the water simply kills one virus and creates another. But it makes the mind feel comfortable.

There will be many new species of animals which are new to the conscious mind, but not new to the Earth. The animal kingdom will live in harmony and peace with mankind. Fear will simply be known as an energy that once existed. Many souls will physically incarnate here to teach life, light, and methods of growing crops which do not take the minerals from the Earth, but give back minerals to the Earth.

There will not be such contraptions, as you would call them, or small boxes some people call a home. Each would share land. There would not be ownership of land. How can you own an entity called Earth? Many think they do, and think it gives them power. But truly they do not own land. There will be no greed, no neighbor arguing with another neighbor over which square foot of soil is on their deed. Such restrictions mankind holds! Such limitations mankind holds! Mankind will know how to live in peace. There will be no weapons, for there will be no need for weapons. There will be no need for pain. War will be obsolete.

Within this New Age, the Golden Age, there will again be established a line of communication with the Universe. Knowledge and experiences will be shared with many planetary systems which also carry physical life. The Earth will not be isolated, as it is now, from so many of the brothers and sisters who live not far from your planet. Lands of rainbows will exist, but the rainbows will not be an isolated incident as they are now. Where you see rainbows now is a small example of what your skies would look like at all times, and what your waters would look like at all times.

Some call this the Millennium. Millennium simply means a thousand years. It is an evolutionary cycle which mankind has been experiencing. The returning again to the land of Lemuria is the New Age. Mankind felt it needed to experience good and bad, positive and negative, pain and joy. The path of learning has been created. You need not re-travel the roadway of pain.

So many of your corporate religions constantly preach the return of the man Jesus to save the world. The confusion here is that the coming of the Christed-energy is not limited to one physical man. The Christed-energy is a universal energy which creates universal peace and tranquility. That is the Light which we referred to previously, the Light which everyone on Earth will be able to see. There is coming the graduation of your planet.

The Earth is moving and shifting its vibration into a vibration of harmony.

The peaceful tranquility which can come from sitting outdoors, listening to the sounds of water, the singing of birds, would be an everyday occurrence because you would not know or give credit to anything lesser. This energy exists within everyone and in all locations of the Earth. The harshness of the sun which you can feel upon the skin will not exist because there will be much more moisture in the atmosphere. You will not have to worry about the skin being burned from the radiation of the sun.

Children will play with children, regardless of the color of their skin. It is difficult for some minds to comprehend this because of such judgments they have embedded in their minds through traditions. Adults will play as children. They will not separate, as you do in this culture, where they must run off to the great office and work, then return to a family. The family will work together. There will not be a separation in family units. There will not be great jealousy in the family units.

The trees will be of a much greater vibrancy in color than ones you see now. The colors you see now in the reflection of the waters, in the clouds at sunset, will be magnified thousands of times. There will be the colors, the vibrancy, the life, the life-force, and the God-force which will exist.

Many of the souls who held a physical body which departed the physical because of the many shifts of cleansing of this Earth will have the opportunity to come back to this Earth again in physical form. It will be at a much higher vibration so they may release their attachments of the traditional mind and evolve into their own individual graduation of peace and harmony.

We well know there are many reading this message who hold the concept in their mind that this would be an ideal world to live in, but they cannot see it happening. Those who make these statements are the ones who are so locked into their own minds and limitations that they will need to experience tribulation because they do not give credit to life. They do not give credit to the power of the Universe and the power of the God-force which can alter and change in the blinking of an eye. Whether they believe it or not will not alter the fact that it will occur. It will occur. It is already beginning to occur.

And when they come to recognize, when they stop fighting, when they stop arguing, peace can truly exist within their own minds. Many people do not even give peace a chance to exist because of their stubborn intellect, because of their ego, and because of fear, fear of survival, or fear of not being respected by their community which does not know peace.

It does not matter whether you believe in this message or not. It is and will be occurring. We spoke a message two thousand years ago regarding events to occur which would lead up to this. Many of them are now occurring.

Again, we will say that all that is worth living for, all that is worth growing for, all that is worth releasing the pain in the mind for, all this is for the pursuit of true joy, of freedom, the freedom to be what you are, the freedom to know who you are, the freedom to love yourself as well as loving everyone who exists, the freedom to allow yourself to enter into the New Age, the Golden Age, the freedom to live life to the fullest without limitation, without becoming lost, without again going to sleep (and we are not speaking of physical sleep), the freedom to walk in nature and smell a flower, the freedom to play with children, the freedom to drink the waters, the freedom to eat the bread of life, the freedom to explore the concept that the only limitation which exists is what you believe in, the freedom to know that life is eternal, and the freedom to know that you do not need to give credit to worrying, to being afraid.

Know that true joy is truly yours. All you need do, my friends, is ask for it. Good day.

978-0-595-47415-8
0-595-47415-2

Printed in the United States
105301LV00013B/64/P